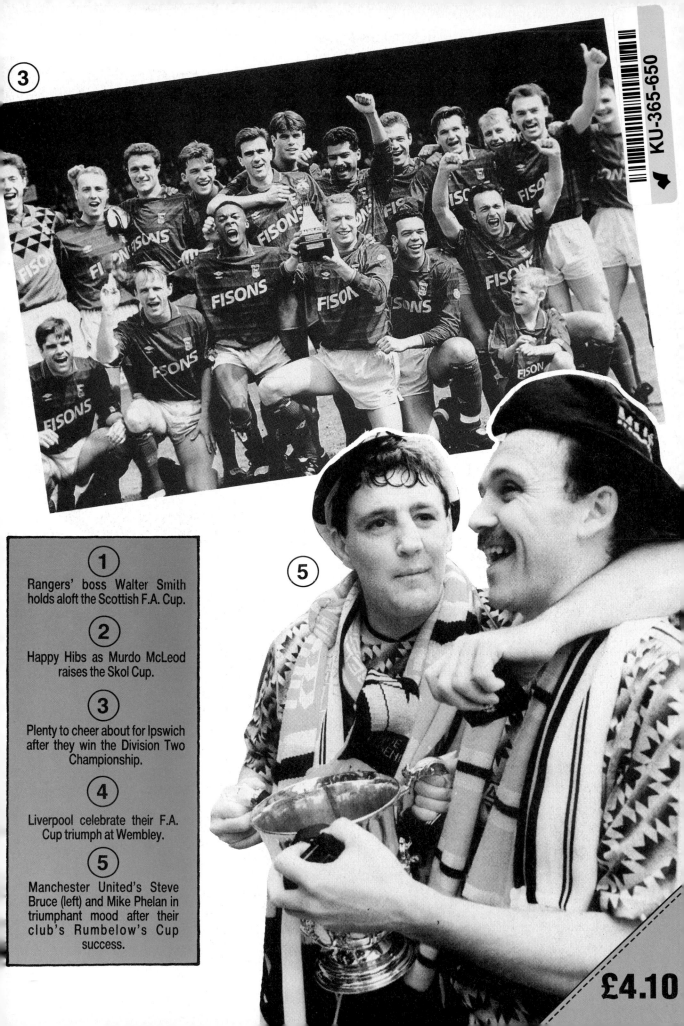

3

1
Rangers' boss Walter Smith holds aloft the Scottish F.A. Cup.

2
Happy Hibs as Murdo McLeod raises the Skol Cup.

3
Plenty to cheer about for Ipswich after they win the Division Two Championship.

4
Liverpool celebrate their F.A. Cup triumph at Wembley.

5
Manchester United's Steve Bruce (left) and Mike Phelan in triumphant mood after their club's Rumbelow's Cup success.

5

£4.10

The Topical Times

FOOTBALL BOOK

Contents

JOINING Celtic at the beginning of 1992 really was a dream come true for me. When the offer of a swap deal between myself and Tony Cascarino first came up I had no qualms about leaving Chelsea after just nine months at Stamford Bridge.

My move from Motherwell to London hadn't worked out quite as well as I'd hoped.

It was just after I'd captained Motherwell to their Scottish Cup win over Dundee United that the bid from Chelsea came in.

My contract was almost up at Fir Park and I'd made up my mind months in advance that I would be leaving the club. Winning the Scottish Cup didn't alter my thinking in any way.

There were a few clubs showing interest, but I plumped for Chelsea because they showed a lot of ambition and Ian Porterfield was trying to build a strong team.

On the pitch, I enjoyed my brief spell with Chelsea in the English First Division. It was great to visit unfamiliar grounds and play against players I'd never faced before.

However, off the field, things didn't work out quite so well. My wife and I couldn't really settle in the south and we missed our families quite a lot.

So when Celtic came in with their swap deal offer involving Tony Cascarino I was delighted to accept.

The great thing was I found it extremely easy slotting in at Parkhead

COMING CELTIC'S WAY!

e claim of Parkhead star TOM BOYD.

and I think that's largely due to the six happy years I spent at Motherwell.

Because of my time at Fir Park under Tommy McLean, I knew the Scottish scene inside out — and that included everyone at Celtic.

Unlike players who are totally alien to the Scottish game — like Tony Cascarino — I've always known Celtic's style and how good their players were.

I was also a Celtic fan as a boy and knew a lot about the history of the club. That's why it seemed so easy settling in.

Another bonus was the fact we didn't have a house in England to sell. Getting rid of property can be a real hassle, especially when you're trying to do your best for your new team.

I'm now playing for a team that's expected to win every game and under manager Liam Brady and his assistant Tommy Craig, we fortunately seem to be doing that most weeks.

It was a major disappointment not to win something in my first season at Parkhead — even though I only played for the last few months.

Although we had a lengthy unbeaten run in the Premier Division from the turn of the year, it still wasn't enough to prevent Old Firm rivals Rangers capturing their fourth title in a row.

In the end, we stumbled in our last game at home to Hibs which allowed Hearts to finish as runners-up.

We also lost to an Ally McCoist goal in the Scottish Cup semi-final against Rangers. Even though they were down to ten men early on, after David Robertson had been sent off for a foul on Joe Miller, we didn't perform particularly well and didn't pose them enough problems.

Naturally, after finishing third in the League and getting knocked out of the Cup, everybody at the club thought our chances of European football had been scuppered.

That's when UEFA stepped in at the end of May and announced that we were to be given one of the vacant Euro places caused by Germany's reunification and the general unrest in Eastern Europe.

We would have preferred to have qualified on our own achievements, but you can't look a gift horse in the mouth and the big Euro nights of Parkhead are vital to the players, officials and supporters.

I was probably the happiest player at Celtic when I heard the news because I hadn't played in Europe at club level before.

I missed out on Motherwell's European Cup-Winners' Cup campaign because I'd joined Chelsea and by the time I'd moved to Parkhead, Celtic had been knocked out of the UEFA Cup.

Another incentive to return to Scotland was that it would improve my international chances.

Andy Roxburgh is a very fair coach to work under and he travels the length and breadth of the country to keep an eye on all his players, but it's always an advantage to be playing on the boss's doorstep!

I've now played a handful of games for my country, and I'd like to think that playing for a successful Celtic side can only enhance my chances.

With Maurice Malpas virtually an ever-present in the Scotland team at left back, and young Rangers defender David Robertson also challenging, there's no shortage of competition for that position.

But I've played a number of games on the left side of midfield for Andy Roxburgh and I'm happy to do a job there when required. It pays to be a little bit versatile in football and there's no greater honour than playing for your country.

On the club front, nothing would give me greater pleasure than to help fill the trophy room at Celtic Park.

The club has gone too long without winning trophies on a regular basis. Their last great year was the centenary season of '87-'88 when they won the League and Cup double.

There's no doubt in my mind that the success will come back to this club sooner rather than later.

In his first season at the club Liam Brady made a huge improvement to the performances on the pitch. I think his efforts deserve some sort of reward.

7

PETER BEARDSLEY

EVERTON

How Sweden '92 hit the headlines.

Fairytale Finish!

THOMAS HASSLER
GERMANY

JEAN-PIERRE PAPIN
FRANCE

SANDWICHED between the passion, romance and atmosphere of World Cup Italia '90 and the expected razzamatazz, hi-tech and glamour of World Cup '94 in America, the European Championships in Sweden were always going to suffer in comparison.

'Small is beautiful' was the hosts' boast prior to Euro '92. The four stadiums used for the eight-nation competition were low capacity. The Final in the Ullevi Stadium, Gothenburg could house only 35,000.

Compare that to the big capacity grounds Italy used and you can see that for atmosphere the Swedes were never going to match the spine-tingling fervour generated in the World Cup two years ago.

But the tournament did manage to

MARCO VAN BASTEN
HOLLAND

conjure up games, names and incidents to live in the memory alongside those from more glamorous occasions.

It even managed to throw up a sequence of events that ultimately led to an unlikely final — and an even more unlikely winner!

Germany, who had already been thrashed 3-1 in their group by Holland, met Denmark, the unprepared no-hopers, who were let into the championships by the back door when war-torn Yugoslavia were banned just 10 days before the tournament began!

To the astonishment of everybody — except perhaps the Danes — the cup went to the rank outsiders!

But it wasn't just the top teams who were overshadowed by the events of Sweden '92. Many of the famous individual names of Europe were eclipsed by players who were unknown to most of us before the championships.

With Lothar Matthaus injured, little Thomas Hassler grabbed the stage for Germany. Remember his free-kicks against the CIS and Sweden?

Dennis Bergkamp of Holland outshone his more illustrious team-mates Ruud Gullit and Marco Van Basten.

Sweden's own Tomas Brolin and Jan Eriksson with their goal contributions delighted the host nation. And Denmark's Flemming Povlsen became an overnight star.

There were individual and team disappointments too. Gary Lineker and England. And, although Jean-Pierre Papin scored twice, his French team-mates disappointed and also revealed a nastier side to their character as they crashed out at the group stage, kicking and head-butting their way home.

One of the most lingering memories from Italia '90 was the excitement and heartache of the penalty shoot-out. Euro '92 threw up its own equally tense mixture of joy and despair.

Who could forget Manchester United and Denmark's Peter Schmeichel saving Marco Van Basten's penalty in the semi-final? The Dutchman, whose goals had won Holland the trophy in 1988, effectively sending the joint favourites home early due to the miss.

Yes, small it may have been, but the European Championships in Sweden didn't short change anyone on the drama front.

SIX SAD DAYS!

That was England's European Championship campaign.

ENGLAND flew out to Sweden last June expecting to push Holland and Germany for the European crown. Graham Taylor's squad travelled home after just six days of the tournament with no wins, one goal, bottom of their group and in total confusion.

The England manager couldn't decide which tactics to use, couldn't settle on which players would put the various game plans into operation, Gary Lineker couldn't score, and the one man who might have injected some flair was in Italy awaiting the start of his new career with Lazio.

The nation cried out for Paul Gascoigne, as his international colleagues muddled through Taylor's confusion of systems and failed to make any impact.

But Gazza's injury was only one of a catalogue of mishaps that threw Taylor's plans into disarray.

The first inkling that all wouldn't be smooth in England's preparations came three weeks before the tournament began.

Injury removed Liverpool's promising right-back Rob Jones from Graham Taylor's plans. Jones had been ear-marked for the number two shirt in Sweden.

Still, Arsenal's Lee Dixon was a more than capable deputy with international experience behind him. However, days after being named in Taylor's party for the championships, he injured himself on a training run near his home.

Forty-seven times capped Gary Stevens was drafted in and England's squad of 20 was duly registered with UEFA.

Then England entered what proved to be a fateful last warm-up game against Finland.

After just 11 minutes of the friendly in Helsinki, John Barnes ruptured his Achilles tendon and was out of the European Championships. After 45 minutes Gary Stevens stayed in the dressing-room with a stress fracture of his foot and was also out. And after 90 minutes — although it wasn't reported until three days later — Mark Wright came off the pitch with a sore Achilles heel.

Graham Taylor sweated on UEFA allowing him to alter his original squad of 20. Forty-eight hours before jetting to Malmo for the opening matches in Euro 92, it was announced that Manchester City's Keith Curle and Andy Sinton of Queens Park Rangers would be allowed to come in as late replacements.

England, however, were destined not to travel to Sweden with their full quota of players. As the players gathered on the Sunday morning of June 7 at a Luton hotel, the news broke that Mark Wright was injured.

Was the story true? Wright hadn't been seen as the squad gathered and his England suit was still hanging on the rail in one of the hotel rooms.

A clearly annoyed Taylor told the Press that he hadn't been informed of Wright's injury until the evening previous! Wright didn't fly to Malmo that day with the official party and five days later he was written off for the tournament and UEFA refused to

allow Tony Adams to replace him.

In the meantime England's fit 19 players had begun the European Championships.

Graham Taylor had said on the morning of the opening match against Denmark in Malmo that in terms of the tournament he 'expected to win'.

In their hotel in the university city of Lund, 20 miles from Malmo, his confident message to the fans back home was, "Put your feet up in front of the telly and have a good time."

In the event, the width of a post in the Malmo Stadium saved Taylor from choking on his words in front of a 26,000 crowd and millions of TV watchers in England.

Having announced prior to the Finals that the flat back four system that had been employed by England had won nothing for 26 years, that's exactly the formation he sent out to face the Danes.

The Danes revelled in their unexpected late inclusion in the championships at the expense of banned Yugoslavia. England couldn't trouble a defence that included one-time Manchester United player John Sivebaek and ex-Aston Villa man Kent Nielsen. Thus Manchester United's current 'keeper Peter Schmeichel hardly needed to break sweat.

But sweat his opposite number Chris Woods did when John Jensen struck a shot that eluded him, but bounced back off the post into the safety of the 'keeper's arms.

The 4,000 English fans breathed a sigh of relief. A catastrophic start was averted, it put the jitters into the England ranks and they decided at that stage that they were happy to survive the 90 minutes with a point.

Next came Michel Platini's France. The same Malmo Stadium, the same 0-0 scoreline. But a change to the continental sweeper system and three players from the Denmark game, Keith Curle, Paul Merson and Alan Smith were out.

Again caution was the winner. The French didn't want to lose and England were content to take another point off the favourites to win the group.

There was one moment to cheer in that game — Stuart Pearce's free-kick. Whilst England were a goalpost away from defeat against the Danes, the French were a crossbar away from losing against Taylor's side.

Pearce had just suffered an alleged head butt from France's Basile Boli. The Nottingham Forest left back was ordered to wipe away the blood from his face as the free kick was being lined up. He returned to the pitch in time to crash a scorcher against the bar.

Despite these set-backs England could still go through to the semi-finals if they beat the host nation Sweden in their capital city of Stockholm.

The party flew on from Malmo in confident mood. But the chants of 'What a load of rubbish' and 'All we are saying is give us a goal' were still ringing in their ears from the fans.

Could Gary Lineker break England's goal duck and equal Bobby Charlton's all-time goalscoring record for his country of 49 goals? Even better if the skipper could get two, break the record and take England into the semis and a fitting finale to his international career. He'd announced it would end after the European Championships.

Taylor had changed tactics yet again. Once more there was a flat back four formation with David Platt shifted out of midfield and placed alongside Lineker to help him break that elusive record.

The Rasunda Stadium was alive with the atmosphere which was sadly lacking in Malmo. Here in Stockholm it was more like an English ground, close to the pitch.

The yellow and blue scarves, hats, banners, clothing and faces of the host supporters made a colourful scene, but England dulled their fervour as early as the fourth minute.

Not Lineker equalling Charlton's record, but Lineker crossing for David Platt to strike a

GARY LINEKER

shot home. What a start!

No further headway was made. Lineker never even had a sniff of a chance and the Swedish support, who'd been silenced by Platt's opener, began to grow noisy again. They sensed it wasn't over.

In the second half, Sweden changed their tactics. Arsenal's Anders Limpar was taken off at half-time and replaced by Johnny Ekstrom. England's defence started crumbling under the onslaught.

First Jan Eriksson crashed a free header past Chris Woods then Tomas Brolin conjured up a delightful move that ripped England open and ended with the Swedes' pin-up boy scooping one of the goals of the tournament high into Woods' net. 2-1 to Sweden.

Then came movement on the England bench. Arsenal striker Alan Smith stripped off his tracksuit and the UEFA official on the sideline raised a number to signal who Graham Taylor was taking off.

It was the number 10. Gary

Lineker's! In a desperate last gamble to remain in the championships the England manager took off his leading goalscorer!

"I was trying to buy Gary Lineker another game for England," Taylor was to say afterwards.

But the switch didn't work. Lineker wasn't going to add to his 80 caps and his magnificent international career ended ingloriously. Subbed, no goals to his name in Sweden, stuck forever more one goal behind Bobby Charlton and England out of Euro 92.

The pre-tournament boast that "I expect to win," by Taylor sounded embarrassingly hollow. England were rock bottom of their group. A shapeless ragged outfit confused by a succession of tactical switches.

The World Cup qualifiers are now upon us. Can Graham Taylor drag England up off the floor and go to America in 1994 and repair a tarnished reputation? Time will tell!

PRIDE IN THE JERSEY

THE POWER BEHIND SCOTLAND'S EUROPEAN CHAMPIONSHIPS CHALLENGE.

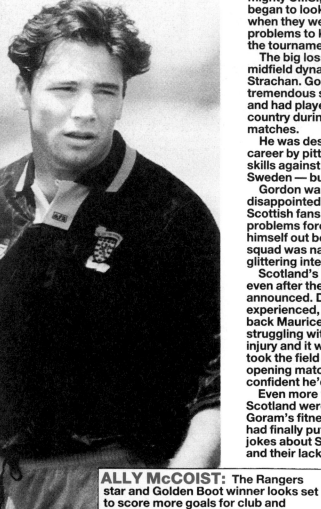

PRIDE in the jersey, that's what pushes Scotland's players on to the kind of exciting displays that made Scotland the talk of the early stages of the European Championships in Sweden during the summer.

Before a ball was kicked in the Championships, Scotland were everybody's fall guys. Unlucky enough to be named in the same group as holders Holland, world champions Germany and the mighty C.I.S., Scotland's task began to look almost impossible when they were hit by injury problems to key players before the tournament had even begun!

The big loss was Leeds United midfield dynamo Gordon Strachan. Gordon had had a tremendous season at club level and had played brilliantly for his country during the qualification matches.

He was desperate to climax his career by pitting his terrier-like skills against Europe's best in Sweden — but it was not to be.

Gordon was every bit as disappointed as the legions of Scottish fans when back problems forced him to rule himself out before the Scotland squad was named. A sad end to a glittering international career.

Scotland's problems continued even after the squad was announced. Dundee United's experienced, dependable full back Maurice Malpas was struggling with an Achilles tendon injury and it wasn't really until he took the field in Scotland's opening match that fans were confident he'd make it!

Even more worrying for Scotland were 'keeper Andy Goram's fitness problems. Andy had finally put a stop to all the jokes about Scottish goalkeepers and their lack of ability with some

RICHARD GOUGH: Tough, uncompromising defender who would be guaranteed a place in most countries' line-ups.

great displays for Rangers and Scotland, but it took painkilling injections in his knees and a last minute fitness programme before he could even think of stepping on the plane for Sweden!

Transfer speculation was another source of worry. Big name players wondering about their future aren't likely to play at the peak of their form and with Paul McStay, Pat Nevin, Dave McPherson and Kevin Gallacher all the subject of transfer speculation as the Championships approached, the doom and gloom merchants were having a field day.

The question posed by several "experts" was whether Scotland would snatch a point or even a goal before boarding the plane back to Glasgow!

Scotland, of course, had other ideas. Fresh from a visit to the USA, which had worked wonders for team spirit, coach Andy Roxburgh was determined that if

ALLY McCOIST: The Rangers star and Golden Boot winner looks set to score more goals for club and country.

his team did fail to make it to the semis, it wouldn't be for want of trying!

But all out effort wasn't enough — quite — when Scotland opened their campaign against Rinus Michels supremely talented Dutch squad. Scotland played a tremendous defensive game, only to fall to a late strike from Holland's Bergkamp. Even the Dutch were surprised by that one!

So it was one game down, no points and a tough job to qualify ahead, but the "Tartan Army" recognised a fighting display when they saw one and gave their heroes a great reception.

If anything, Scotland's next opponents were even tougher. Brilliant going forward and solid at the back, with years of success at the highest level behind them, Germany went into their match against the Scots, brimming with confidence.

But Scotland gave them the

fright of their lives! Throwing caution to the wind, the Scots poured forward in waves. In the end, it was only some great saves by the German'keeper, bad luck — and, to be honest, some dodgy finishing — that stood between Roxburgh's men and a famous victory.

Out of the tournament now and maybe wishing they possessed a world class striker like Van Basten, Scotland were determined to leave Sweden on a winning note — and three goals against a strangely lethargic C.I.S. side soon saw to that.

For midfielder Brian McClair that tremendous victory was definitely one for the scrapbook. Brian had scored goals throughout his career. Some great performances for his first senior club, Motherwell, caught Celtic's interest and he went on to become a big favourite and top striker with the Parkhead club.

Following a move to Manchester United, the goals just kept on flowing and Brian is now a top performer in manager Alex Ferguson's all star squad.

"So why can't he score goals for Scotland?" asked the Tartan Army and with twenty-five games for his country under his belt without a goal before the C.I.S. game, it was a fair question!

McClair knew that even without goals he was still doing a job for Scotland, otherwise the manager wouldn't have picked him! But that didn't mean he'd given up hope of finally hitting the back of the net.

Happily for Brian and Scotland, the long wait came to an end during the C.I.S. match — with a little help from a deflection — and the look of joy on his face as he turned away from the goal in triumph said it all. At last, he had scored for his country!

The Tartan Army joined in the celebrations, just as they had throughout the tournament. Win, lose or draw, they were out to enjoy their time in Sweden, without a hint of trouble.

Bagpipes, kilts — and even Viking helmets — the Scottish fans weren't easily missed, but at the end of the day they emerged as superb ambassadors for their country, giving tremendous support for their side, but always aware that football is, after all, only a game.

Even the Swedish police joined in the fun. As the fans relaxed and enjoyed the atmosphere of one of the world's premier footballing occasions, so did the police.

One of the sights of the tournament just had to be the Swedish motorbike police

escorting the Scotland team bus to the C.I.S. match. To a man, they wore Scotland jerseys!

Now Scotland are battling to win a place in the World Cup Finals in the USA in 1994, with their confidence boosted by these stirring displays against Europe's best.

Qualification has got to be on the cards. Five times in a row now, Scotland have made it to the finals and that's one of the best records in world football.

If Scotland do make it to America, they're determined to win through their initial section and launch a real challenge for the trophy.

It may seem to be a tall order, but Scotland are convinced after their displays in Sweden that they can compete with the world's best. And being a small country taking on the giants of world soccer doesn't mean failure is guaranteed.

After all, just take a look at Denmark's tremendous performances in Sweden . . .

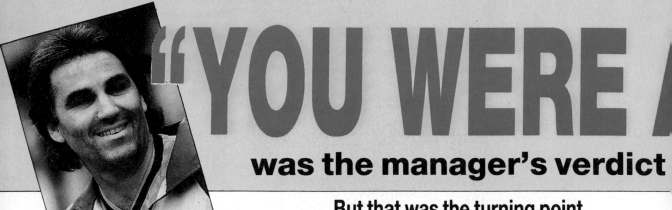

But that was the turning point for IAN HOLLOWAY (Q.P.R.)

LAST season was by far my best and for that I've got to thank Rangers manager Gerry Francis. My career has taken off ever since I met him. Yet the first time he saw me play, Gerry thought I was rubbish!

I was with Brentford at the time, having joined them from Wimbledon. I must admit I was having a bad spell. Moving to London from Bristol Rovers had become a nightmare.

My fiancee had developed cancer, and I went down with a mystery virus, later diagnosed as glandular fever.

I just really wanted to get back home. Gerry Francis had just taken over at Rovers, and was looking for a winger. My mate Gary Penrice, who was with Rovers, recommended me.

Gerry came to watch me at Brentford. I was awful. So bad I was taken off and subbed.

But amazingly, Gerry was still interested. He approached me about signing for Rovers. I couldn't believe it.

I said to him, 'How come you still want to sign me, when I was playing such rubbish?'

Gerry replied, 'You're right. You were awful. But I think I can make you a good player.'

How could I refuse the offer?

My form was poor at that time because of my illness. It had drained everything out of me.

I believe I picked it up soon after I joined Wimbledon. I felt strangely lethargic, which is not like me. I kept going for tests, but they all showed up blank.

At the same time my girlfriend Kim was diagnosed as suffering from cancer of the lymph-gland. She was back in Bristol, and all the dashing backwards and forwards took its toll.

I went down with every germ going round. My form was rubbish.

Worrying about Kim didn't help matters. I wasn't much use to Wimbledon.

Dave Bassett was manager at the time, and he was very sympathetic. He thought a change of scenery would help, and let me join Brentford on loan.

It was while playing for Brentford that I went back to see my own doctor in Bristol for more tests. One day I got an urgent phone call to say he had pin-pointed my trouble. It was glandular fever.

The doctor wanted me to stop playing immediately, or risk serious consequences. The trouble was Brentford manager Frank McLintock needed me to play the last three games of the season, because of injuries to other players.

I rested right through the summer, but even when I re-started training, I quickly became exhausted. The illness had taken so much out of me.

Overall it took me the best part of two years to recover. I was still well short of full fitness when Gerry Francis signed me.

But once back in Bristol things just got better and better for me. Kim had recovered well after lengthy treatment, and we got married. And under the guidance of Gerry and coach Kenny Hibbitt, my game made steady progress.

They switched me from the wing to a midfield role. With two of the best midfield players of their day to help me, I couldn't fail to learn.

Even so it was still a surprise last year, when Gerry Francis asked me to join him at Queens Park Rangers. I didn't know if I was good enough for the First Division.

Gerry said it was for me to prove that I could handle it. But I didn't expect to get in the side.

RAY WILKINS

My chance came when Ray Wilkins was injured in the first game of the season. I really felt I needed more time to get used to the speed of thought in the First Division, but I found myself thrown in at the deep end.

To start with, I tried too hard to play like Ray. I attempted too many difficult things, which was crazy, because I'll never be able to pass the ball like Ray.

But when Gary Penrice joined us from Villa, he helped me out again. He advised me to keep things simple, and play the easy ball.

VFUL!"

Gary told me that his Villa colleague Kevin Richardson had won most of the top honours in the game, at Everton and Arsenal, by doing the simple things well.

After that, things seemed to fall into place for me. When Ray Wilkins was fit to return to the Rangers side, it wasn't me who made way for him. I've gained an awful lot from playing with Ray.

I've always been a 100 miles an hour player, but playing alongside Ray has helped to calm me down. I've seen how cool and casual he is on the ball.

So now I say to myself, 'hang on — there's more time than you think.'

It's a pleasure to play in the team. There's so much talent in the squad. I believe Rangers can win honours in the next year or two.

Gerry Francis has a particular system. He turned around Bristol Rovers completely. They were a struggling Third Division side when he joined, but he got the club into Division Two, and kept it there. It wasn't a fluke. His methods will pay dividends at QPR. He is a winner.

It took a while for the players at QPR to adjust to his system. Early on they weren't quite sure what they were doing. Now everybody has mastered it, and we are a match for any side.

It's great for me to be playing in the Premier League. When I was in Bristol, I honestly thought that time had passed me by as far as top flight football was concerned.

It just shows you what football can be like. It's a roller-coaster, and you have to take the ups with the downs.

I'm still proud of Bristol football. People in London don't know much about it, but there are some good players down there.

When I joined Rangers, people would say 'who did you play for, was it Bristol City?' I'd get annoyed, because the rivalry between Rovers and City in Bristol is just as intense as that between Arsenal and Spurs, or Liverpool and Everton.

It was great for Bristol last season when first Keith Curle, and then Nigel Martyn won full international caps for England. They were both great friends of mine at Rovers.

I was very close to Keith in my first spell at Rovers, before we both moved on. I was best man at his wedding, and we've always kept in touch.

Last summer, when I signed for QPR, Keith invited me to use his house as a home base. He was still at Wimbledon, and I was to live with him until I found a house to buy.

But when I arrived on his doorstep in Surrey, he greeted me with the words, 'I may be joining Manchester City'. Within days he had signed at Maine Road, and moved up to Manchester.

Keith wanted to sell his house right away, so I bought it from him. That was a great help in settling down quickly in London.

My first move to the capital was a bit of a disaster. Now I couldn't be happier — thanks to Gerry Francis.

MARK
BRIGHT
CRYSTAL PALACE

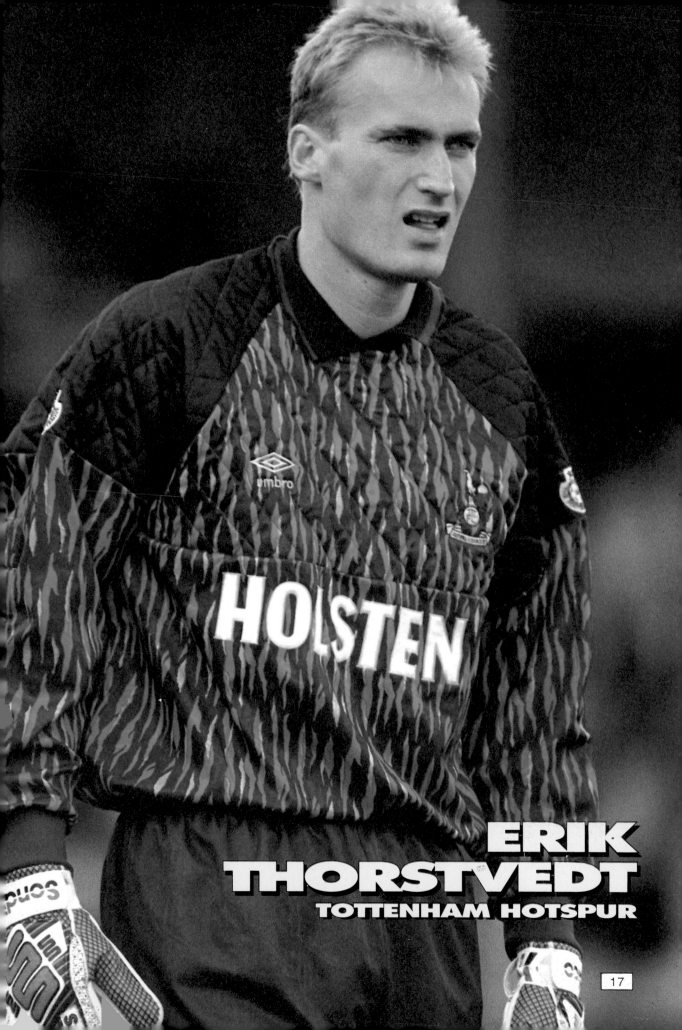

ERIK THORSTVEDT
TOTTENHAM HOTSPUR

17

So you think you know about football...
— now's your chance to prove it!

1. The Spion Kop, an area of covered terracing at several British football grounds (like those at Liverpool and Sheffield Wednesday), is named after the Battle of Spion Kop, which took place during the Boer War in 1900. True or false?

2. Can you name the two clubs with whom Charlton Athletic shared grounds after they left the Valley in 1985.

3. By what name is Edson Arantes do Nascimento better known?

4. In which year did England stage the World Cup?

5. Barnsley, Plymouth Argyle, Port Vale and Tranmere Rovers have one thing in common. What?

6. In which year did the following happen? Aston Villa were Champions of Europe, Spurs won the F.A. Cup and Celtic pipped Aberdeen for the Scottish title.

7. All the following managers have one thing in common. What? Alan Ball (Exeter City), Don Howe (Coventry City), Brian Clough (Nottingham Forest), Jack Charlton (Republic of Ireland), Gerry Francis (Queen's Park Rangers), Phil Neal (Bolton Wanderers). Peter Reid (Manchester City) and Trevor Francis (Sheffield Wednesday).

8. When Bryan Robson was transferred from West Bromwich Albion to Manchester United, he set a new record between British clubs of £1.5 million. In which year did his transfer take place . . . 1980, 1981, 1982?

9. Which club, that wear a yellow and green strip, won the Milk Cup in 1985?

10. Name the two clubs who play at St. James Park and St. James' Park respectively?

11. Which Aberdeen star was voted Scottish Footballer of the Year in 1990?

12. Who did Italy beat to win the 1982 World Cup?

13. In September, 1985, Chris Whyte, currently with Leeds United, scored six goals in a twelve-nil reserve team victory! Which London club was he playing for then?

14. A Second Division manager and one of his players were in the same Spurs side in the mid-eighties. Can you name them both and their current team?

15. Is the minimum length for a football field 100, 110 or 115 yards?

16. Which Fourth Division club played at the Old Show Ground until 1988, then moved to Glanford Park?

17. Who won the Skol League Cup in 1991/92?

18. At the end of the 1990/91 season, which club were Second Division Champions . . . Sheffield Wednesday, Oldham Athletic or West Ham United?

19. Can you remember one of two Italian clubs that Hearts boss Joe Jordan played for during his distinguished career?

20. How much do you know about European soccer? Which countries are the following top clubs from? a. Sparta Prague. b. Porto. c. IKF Gothenburg. d. Real Sociedad. e. Twente Enschede. f. Honved.

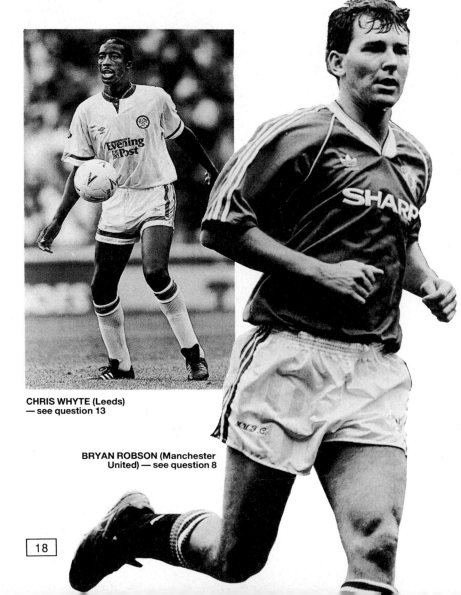

CHRIS WHYTE (Leeds) — see question 13

BRYAN ROBSON (Manchester United) — see question 8

ANSWERS

1. True. 2. Selhurst Park, Crystal Palace and Upton Park, West Ham United. 3. Pele. 4. 1966. 5. They've never played First Division football. 6. 1982. 7. They've all represented England at international level. 8. 1981. 9. Norwich City. 10. Exeter City; Newcastle United. 11. Alex McLeish. 12. West Germany. 13. Arsenal. 14. Glenn Hoddle and Mickey Hazard; Swindon Town. 15. 100 yards. 16. Scunthorpe United. 17. Hibernian. 18. Oldham Athletic. 19. If you said either A.C. Milan or Verona, you're right! 20. a. Czechoslovakia. b. Portugal. c. Sweden. d. Spain. e. Holland. f. Hungary.

THROUGH THE GAP!

Despite the close attentions of Liverpool's ROB JONES, Queens Park Rangers' ANDY SINTON still finds room to manoeuvre.

19

LEAN ON ME!
Leeds' defender TONY DORIGO gets a lift from DAVID HIRST (Sheffield Wednesday).

ROY WEGERLE
BLACKBURN ROVERS

DRESSING ROOM

I had the biggest shock of my career when I sat in Manchester United's dressing-room prior to my debut in the English First Division. It was the opening day of the League season, 45,000 fans were inside Old Trafford, and there were my new team-mates laughing and joking — I couldn't believe it!

A few months into that campaign I, too, was joining in their jokes and banter. I had soon learned my first, and probably one of the most important, lessons of football life in England.

Bryan Robson, Mark Hughes and company taught me that relaxation is the best form of preparation. As the season wore on and the tension rose as our Championship challenge gathered momentum, plus a Rumbelows Cup Final at Wembley thrown in against Nottingham Forest, it proved to be a vital early lesson to learn.

When I was playing in Denmark for Brondby, my pre-match preparation was much more intense. I never gave myself a chance to relax properly.

For two days before a match, my mind would be concentrated solely on playing. It disrupted my

JOKING WAS AN EYE-OPENER –

FOR MANCHESTER UNITED'S
PETER SCHMEICHEL

home life. I wouldn't go shopping with my wife Bente, nor would I play with my children, Kasper and Cecilie. I had thoughts only for the forthcoming match.

By the time I actually got to our dressing-room on match day, I was completely wrapped up in the game. There was no laughing and joking from me. I'd stalk our changing area clutching a football like it was my baby. I was so tensed up I would snap at any team-mate who talked to me.

When I joined United, my new team-mates soon put me straight. They handled the build-up to a game so differently. They all told me that I should learn to calm down. They won't allow me to be straight-faced anymore. If they see anyone looking glum or tense, they get them to snap out of it.

I have also changed my warm-up before a game as well. As part of my preparation for matches in Denmark, I felt I needed to put myself through a vigorous warm-up on the pitch.

I would work-out for 45 minutes virtually non-stop before kick-off! It was a punishing schedule for both myself and the Brondby coach. I would push him to the limit to provide the crosses and shots I felt I needed to prepare properly.

I was soon told to cut that out as well at Old Trafford. Now I only warm-up for about 20 minutes and that's just to get used to the feel of the ball, the pitch and the stadium.

Likewise during the week, I have come to understand that in this country you don't have to exhaust yourself in training to be in top condition for matches.

Footballers don't train as hard during the week in England as they do in my home country Denmark. Over here you don't need to push yourself during the week because there are so many matches to be played. You keep in trim by playing.

I thought I needed a really tough week to be on top of my game. I couldn't come to terms with it at first. I didn't think I was preparing myself properly. I soon found out that playing two games in a week was sufficient. I cannot believe how much I have changed.

I also furthered my footballing education in England by going to watch my local side, Stockport County, in the Third Division.

Stockport's Edgeley Park ground is just three miles from my home and they play a lot of fixtures on a Friday night. So that has given me the opportunity to watch them quite a lot.

I like watching football, so it's not a chore going to extra matches in order to improve my game. Even though County are in the Third, I learned a great deal. Apart from speed and technique, the game in England is the same in the lower divisions as it is in the First.

Obviously the quality of the players is higher in Division One, but the style of game adopted by most clubs is the same in any division. By watching Stockport, I was able to study how and when strikers make a run into the box. I can see clearly where the danger to a goalie comes from. When I am at pitch level, it is very difficult for me to see how build-ups develop.

Even if I could have watched United, it wouldn't have been much use because manager Alex Ferguson is one of the few bosses in England who likes his teams to play a more European style. Ours isn't a typical English game.

So by watching Stockport County I was able to learn and improve my game in England.

It paid off because I was pleased with my introduction to English football. Sure I made some mistakes. The first two goals I conceded in the League for Manchester United against Leeds and Wimbledon were my fault.

I was over-anxious about coming for a cross against Leeds and misjudged it. Against Wimbledon I had heard so much about John Fashanu and his style of game, that I wanted him to know I was around. Unfortunately, that made me come for a ball when I shouldn't have, and he scored.

But I didn't let those errors affect me. I learned a long time ago that dwelling on mistakes only leads to more. Footballers are only human. The key thing is to learn from your errors.

Signing for Manchester United has been everything I hoped it would be. It provided my career with the step up the ladder I needed. I had become stale at Brondby. We were by far the best team in Denmark and I won a number of trophies and championships with them. But over there only a handful of matches a season could be described as hard.

It has been so different at Manchester United. The quality of the First Division is such that there were only a couple of home games at Old Trafford last season that I could say were easy afternoons.

It was a bitter disappointment not to win the Championship last season, but I'm sure we can do it this time around.

KINGSLEY BLACK
NOTTINGHAM FOREST

RIVALS

On opposite sides in the Manchester 'Derby', DAVID WHITE (City) and LEE SHARPE (United) both show the determination that helps make these encounters such a hit with the fans!

IT doesn't seem possible that barely two years ago I nearly gave up football altogether. Now I can't get enough of it.

I can look back on the European Championships with England in Sweden and look forward to the next World Cup campaign, and hopefully, more honours with Arsenal.

For that I can thank my dad. When I told him I was going to chuck it all in, he talked me out of it. Told me to pull myself together, and make the most of my ability.

THANKS, DAD!

that's Arsenal's PAUL MERSON talking.

My dad took me everywhere as a kid — training, matches or kick-abouts in the park. He wasn't prepared to see me throw all that away.

When I won my first full England cap last season, I was almost more pleased for my mum and dad, than for myself. It was a thrill for them, and great for me to be able to pay them back for their help.

Everyone knows I had problems at Highbury a few years ago. I used to think I could play football on a Saturday, and still go out every night in the week. I didn't see anything wrong in that.

But other people did. I used to get picked on. Everyone wanted to wind me up. Every incident got blown up.

I wanted to have a quiet drink, but I couldn't do that. But I couldn't sit at home all day long. That got on my nerves.

It all began to get on top of me. I was going through a nightmare on the pitch. The Arsenal directors were putting pressure on the manager to throw me out.

That's when I talked to my dad about quitting. I fancied going abroad, and finding a place in the sun.

Fortunately he talked me out of it. I haven't looked back since. I've worked hard at my game. Once I decided to carry on, I didn't mess around.

Arsenal manager George Graham has been great. He was under so much pressure to get rid of me, it was unbelievable. But he said 'no' and stuck by me.

I worked every day on the weights with the boss. I didn't have a day off in six months. When the other players had a day off, I went in and did a three mile run.

It has all paid off. These days I feel very fit, very lively. I get stronger as the game gets on.

In the old days I used to get taken off in the last 15-20 minutes of almost every game. Nowadays this period is the best part for me. That's when my strength pays off.

It's been a whirlwind couple of years. Everything has gone well for me since I pulled myself together. I'm on a platform now, and I want to keep going up and up.

It was great to get into the England squad last year. Even better to score my first international goal in Czechoslovakia.

Now I want to build on that. In the long term I would like to establish myself as an England striker.

George Graham has used me in different roles at Highbury in the last couple of years. I've played out wide on the left and the right, and in virtually a midfield role.

It's all been good experience. But I prefer playing up front. I feel I am a goalscorer, and play my best as a front man. I like to take on defenders where it counts — in their penalty-box.

I was really chuffed to get into the England senior squad last season. Now I just hope to stay there. I'm really looking forward to the next few years.

There is so much to play for, with the World Cup qualifying games and all the domestic trophies.

Last season was disappointing for Arsenal. We didn't quite put it together consistently. But the ability is still there. We can win the title again.

There is no bigger club in Britain than Arsenal. Continental football does appeal to me, as it must do to every ambitious footballer, but for the time being, I want to repay Arsenal for sticking by me.

I hope to be playing for Arsenal for several years to come — thanks to my dad.

EYES SHUT — HERE WE GO!

Manchester City's MIKE SHERON closes his eyes and leaps in while JOHN GANNON (Sheffield United) can't bear to look.

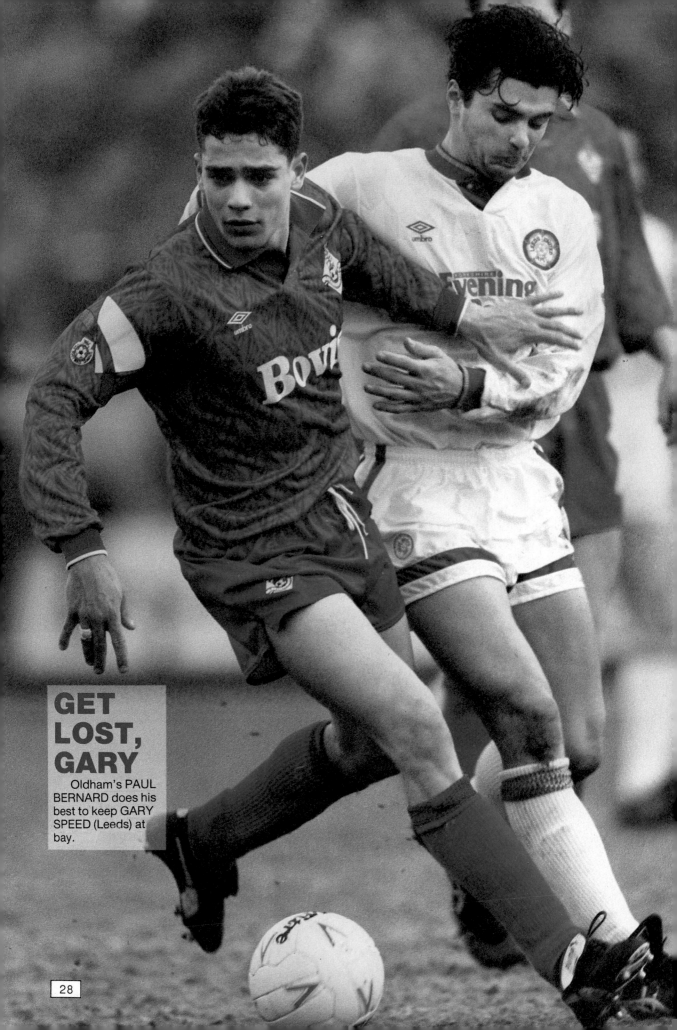

GET LOST, GARY

Oldham's PAUL BERNARD does his best to keep GARY SPEED (Leeds) at bay.

RYAN
GIGGS
MANCHESTER UNITED

29

I'M

DAVID HIRST is a top First Division goalscorer . . . an England Internationalist . . . and carries a multi-million pound price on his head.

All of which is a million miles from the sort of life he would be leading had he not been blessed with the kind of talent which has had all the big clubs casting envious eyes in his direction.

The Sheffield Wednesday striker points out that, had he not made the grade as a footballer, he would probably have spent his days at a coal face, working in the mines of South Yorkshire.

RON ATKINSON

SCORING GOALS
NOT DIGGING COAL!

He grew up in the streets around the coal pits of Barnsley. Many of his mates now work as miners. And when he wants a night out, he often heads for the local working men's club with his father or those same old school chums.

David is proud of that background, and wouldn't like to live in any other environment. Nevertheless, every time he drives home from training and surveys a landscape dotted with the familiar colliery scenes, he offers a silent "Thank you" for the ability which enabled him to escape the life of a miner.

It's a sentiment also repeated regularly by his Dad, who spent years trying to make sure that his lad avoided the job which had long been a family tradition.

"Almost all the men in my family have been miners, and when I was growing up, the pit was the first thing I saw," David recalls. "My father worked there himself. Having experienced at first hand the conditions down there, he was determined to make sure that I didn't follow him.

"From the very earliest age, I can remember him warning me strongly against being a miner. I think he'd have been happy to see me working at anything, as long as it wasn't down the pit.

"But for all that, I'm convinced that I'd still have ended up as a miner if I hadn't been good enough to play professional football.

"I'm glad things turned out the way they did. Though working conditions have improved a lot since my Dad first started dissuading me from that life, I now realise how lucky I am. Having said that, I would never turn my back on the community which brought me up or the people I knew in those younger days. I still love that part of Yorkshire and have kept all my own friends.

"I often nip down to the local near my parents' home to meet my mates, or play snooker or pool with my Dad at the working men's club. They're a terrific crowd. The sort that would make sure that I never became too big for my boots.

"They'd soon give me plenty of stick and bring me back to earth.

Sheffield Wednesday's DAVID HIRST tells how his football skills changed his whole life.

TREVOR FRANCIS

Not that they'd ever need to though, because I've always regarded myself as one of them anyway."

Hirst became an England player during England's tour Down Under in the summer of 1991. Having made his debut against Australia, he then scored his first international goal after coming on as a substitute against New Zealand.

"That trip gave me a terrific boost," he goes on. "It was an acknowledgement that I could play a bit, and after scoring that goal I came home with no end of confidence.

"I reckon I've progressed tremendously during the past few years, but I wouldn't have come so far if it hadn't been for the influence of my last two managers at Sheffield Wednesday.

"Ron Atkinson put me in the side and persisted with me even when I wasn't scoring goals. Until he became the manager at Hillsborough — in February 1989 — I'd never been given a decent run in the team. But Ron showed a lot of faith in me. He gave me the confidence to play my natural game, free from any worries about how long my chance would last.

"He told me, 'All right, son, you're not scoring goals. But at least you are playing well enough for the team, and helping us to do well.' That took a huge weight off my mind. I was able to play in matches thinking, 'As long as I do nothing wrong, I don't think the boss will leave me out next week.' When you have that assurance, it makes the game a lot easier to play.

"If, on the other hand, you are playing with the worry that you might be dropped to accommodate somebody else, even though your general game has been okay, then you struggle from the start. That happened to me often before big Ron's arrival.

"By the time he left to join Aston Villa, I had repaid his faith with goals and my all-round game had improved immensely.

"Trevor Francis took over as boss and, in turn, he has also helped me a lot. With his background as a top striker himself, he has regular sessions with the Wednesday forwards. In fact you couldn't have anybody better to learn from.

"Trevor has added a lot of little touches to my game, without having to drill them into me. I've come off the field at the end of matches having done something a bit different and, though it might not have been something we worked on at length, I'd know Trevor put it there.

"Probably because he has such great natural ability himself, it rubs off. The fact that I can react without thinking about it says a lot for the way in which he has improved my awareness of situations and the instinctive way in which I handle them."

WARREN
BARTON
WIMBLEDON

DAVID
BURROWS
LIVERPOOL

33

I'LL SHOW 'EM!

STEVE McMAHON had a double spur to drive him on when he donned a Manchester City jersey for the first time last season.

The 17-times-capped England internationalist arrived at Maine Road after a £900,000 transfer from Liverpool on Christmas Eve and immediately got down to the task of running the midfield for his new club.

A Player of the Month award at the end of his first full month of League action showed that he meant business.

McMahon had left Anfield seeking a new challenge to pump fresh impetus into his career. The prospect of helping re-establish City as one of the country's top clubs was exactly

That was the vow of Manchester City's STEVE McMAHON.

the sort of task which appealed.

But if Steve needed any other motivation, he only needed to listen to the cynics who questioned his motives for wishing to leave Liverpool in the first place.

According to some, he was taking a step down the

GRAEME SOUNESS

footballing ladder as he began to wind down his first class career.

So, with every meaty tackle and every defence-splitting pass after pulling on that light blue jersey, McMahon was throwing those accusations back in the faces of the doubters.

"I know exactly the sort of thing that was levelled at me after I left," says Steve. "Because Liverpool have enjoyed so much success, some people were asking why I would want to leave. They jumped to the conclusion that I was looking for a cushy number during the latter part of my career.

"That's not true, of course. It's not as if things weren't going well for me at Anfield. I still had almost four years to run of my Liverpool contract, I was playing regularly in the first team and had just done a stint as team captain before my transfer.

"If I'd stayed, I believe I would still have had plenty to offer the club. Even if I'd been out of favour, I wouldn't have given up without a fight. I'd have battled to win my way back into the front line.

"But though at the time my personal situation seemed secure at Anfield there is no substitute for being happy in your work, and I didn't feel content about the way things were going there.

"There had been so many changes within a short period it didn't seem like the old Liverpool any more. There was no longer a sense of continuity.

"I went to see manager Graeme Souness, told him my feelings, and soon I was on my way to City."

McMAHON is now with his fourth big club. Spells with Everton and Aston Villa preceded his six years at Liverpool, where he won three League Championships, two FA Cup winners' medals and all his England caps.

Now he hopes that his association with Manchester City will also be productive in terms of silverware.

He goes on: "I don't want anybody to think that I've come here believing I'll have a cushy number. I don't consider for a minute that I've dropped down a peg by coming to Maine Road.

"This is a big club and the potential is enormous. I feel as though I've been given a new lease of life in being asked to play a part in helping City go back to the top.

"I rate this club as highly as I did Liverpool, though it's a different type of challenge. Liverpool were used to winning all the big prizes, whereas City have been striving for a number of years to regain their place at the top of the football tree.

"But it's the sort of challenge which has given me a tremendous lift.

"I know there are people around who will say that, because I've passed the age of 30, I'm also past my prime.

"But that idea is a fallacy. I have a lot of life and plenty of pride left, and I intend to prove it. I'm convinced I still have some of my best years ahead of me.

"City obviously think so too, because they took over the contract I had at Liverpool. They must feel I'll still be at the top in three years' time when it expires. I have no intention of letting them down."

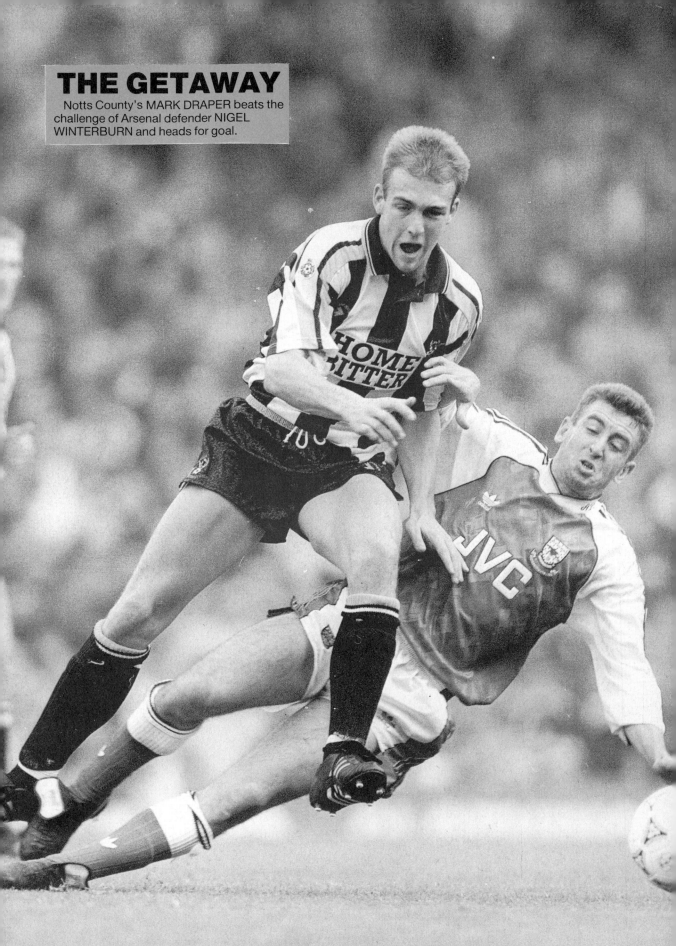

THE GETAWAY

Notts County's MARK DRAPER beats the
challenge of Arsenal defender NIGEL
WINTERBURN and heads for goal.

JAN STEJSKAL
QUEENS PARK RANGERS

THE name of Liverpool has been associated with some of the biggest stars in Europe. The Merseyside club have never baulked at splashing out vast sums of money to bring in the best players.

In the past, few homegrown players made it into the first team on a regular basis, instead spending years languishing in the reserves before moving on to another club.

As the best club team in Europe, Liverpool were criticised for their unwillingness and inability to foster their own talent, but those days seem to be leaving the famous ground.

Nowadays the stars don't sleep so easy in their first team berths. The new generation is waiting in the wings.

Steve McManaman (20) and Mike Marsh (23) are two young homegrown players who found themselves thrust into the limelight as they made their first team debuts season, much earlier than anyone would have anticipated.

Hit by crippling long-term injuries to his senior staff, manager Graeme Souness was forced to throw his youngsters in at the deep end to replace the likes of Ronnie Whelan, John Barnes and Ian Rush. Instead of being overwhelmed by the whole experience, the New Kids on the Kop proved to be a revelation.

Marsh was praised for his ability to win the ball in a League

Steve McManaman

the young

where he might have been expected never even to see it, while McManaman's trickery thrilled the fans and sent experienced full-backs home with resolutions to work on their game.

And with more youth talent like Steve Harkness, Don Hutchison, (both 21), Rob Jones (20) and Jamie Redknapp (19) — all bought cheaply from smaller clubs — Liverpool's standards don't seem to be in any danger of slipping when the famous Old Guard retire.

Bright new stars from the Anfield Football Academy

Says England Youth midfielder Harkness, "I was prepared to wait until the season's end before staking a claim, but with so many players on the treatment table I was given an unexpected chance.

"It is difficult adjusting to the different demands of playing in the first team. I know I'm inexperienced, but I'm putting it right with every passing game."

Jones, bought from Crewe in October 1991 for £300,000, made an immediate impact. On September 28 he played in front of 3,126 fans at Crewe's tiny stadium. Eight days later he made his League debut for Liverpool in front of a 44,997 crowd at Old Trafford, with millions more watching on television, and was universally praised for his cool handling of red-hot United winger Ryan Giggs. Then on February 19th he won his first full cap for England against France.

The Liverpool young guns' ability to handle even the cauldron of a packed Old Trafford bodes well for the future.

Says Rob, "The young guys here are all great hopes for the future. Like myself, in a few years time they'll be looking to make sure they have a regular place in the Liverpool side."

Ironically, it was the departure of Kenny Dalglish, a manager who brought so much success to Liverpool, that gave the youngsters their chance.

Harkness, who spent two years in the reserves without a first team call-up, admits Dalglish told him his chances of a run in the first team were slim as long as he was in charge. It was only when the Scotsman left and number two Ronnie Moran took over that Steve got in the side. And Mike Marsh was ready to leave Anfield after four years in the reserves when Souness gave him his big chance.

Redknapp, too, knew what to expect when he arrived.

"I knew I would have to spend time in the reserves," says Jamie. "But I was prepared to do that because I came to Liverpool to learn.

"I expected to wait a long time before I broke through to the first eleven. But I knew I couldn't come to a better football club to improve my game.

"I was expecting maybe a couple of years in the reserves before I thought I'd be knocking on the senior door. That was how it was looking under Kenny Dalglish in my first few months.

"But when Graeme Souness arrived, the attitude changed. All the young lads suddenly realised if you were good enough and gave the boss 100 per cent, it didn't matter who you were or how old you were he would give you a chance."

League matches aren't the only place where the youngsters have the chance to shine. The four-foreigners rule, now operating in European competitions, offers them a lifeline even when the senior men are all fit.

Redknapp continues, "I made my debut against Auxerre in France in the UEFA Cup and have trained with the senior squad ever since.

"I've learnt so much at Anfield. You couldn't fail to improve here though. You are treated in such a way by the coaching staff you can only learn and get better."

At the start of the season the performances of the young players even overshadowed the displays of Graeme Souness' other, more illustrious signings.

Although their places in the Liverpool team are not assured, that's a lesson bigger names than theirs have had to learn. The good news for Reds' fans is that a whole new group of extremely talented players is coming through the ranks. The Liverpool of the 90's promises to be just as exciting as the Liverpool of the 80's.

guns

This page
left to right
Mike Marsh
Rob Jones
Jamie Redknapp

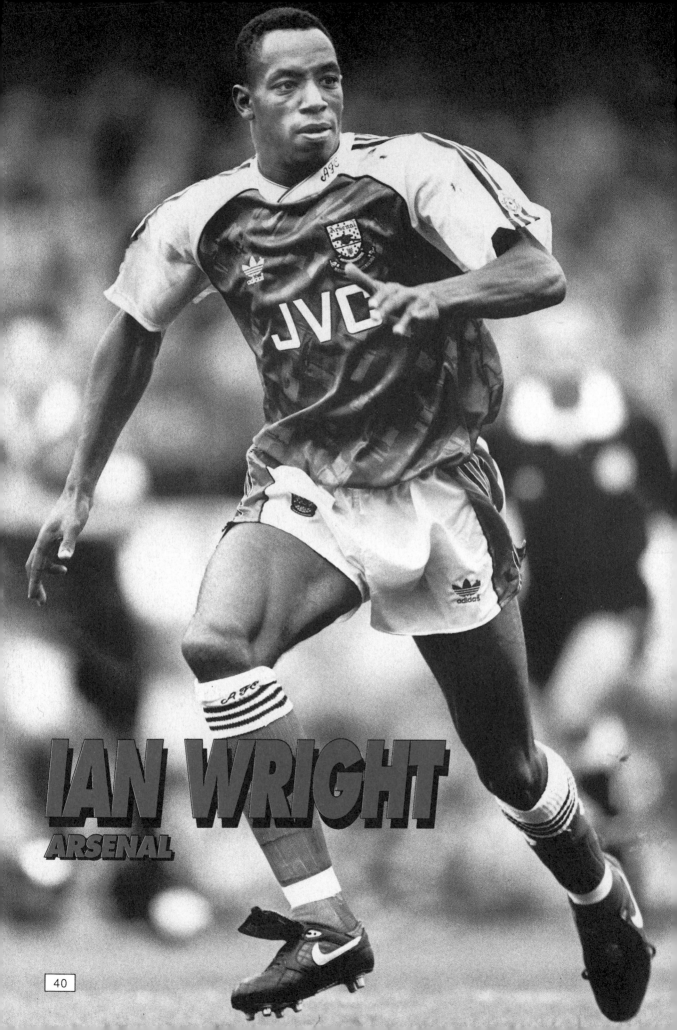

IAN WRIGHT
ARSENAL

NIGEL PEARSON
SHEFFIELD WEDNESDAY

TUG O' WAR

Wimbledon's JOHN FASHANU finds that try as he might he can't break the grip of PAUL McGRATH (Aston Villa).

City Slicker . . .

. . . that was Sheffield United's PAUL ROGERS

THE penalty area of a First Division club's training ground is one of the last places you'd expect to hear a telephone ring.

But when such a noise resounds around the Sheffield United practice pitch it's a sure sign Paul Rogers is about to take a penalty. It's also pretty certain that the ringing is coming from Paul's team-mates.

It's all part of the winding-up process that the Blades' midfield signing from non-League Sutton United has had to endure since his £25,000 switch to full-time football from another high-pressure occupation last February.

"Before signing for Sheffield United I was a commodities broker in the City of London," he says. "It was very busy and with a fair bit of pressure.

"I worked in the City for seven years, joining a brokerage firm straight from school as a messenger and ending up as an actual broker. While there I would trade interest rates, currencies and metals, such as gold and silver.

"But all through my time in the City I wanted to be a professional footballer. That explains why it took me all of ten minutes to make up my mind whether or not to sign for Sheffield United.

"For the first few months after joining the club it seemed like I was on holiday. I couldn't believe I was getting up at nine in the morning, then doing a few hours training before being home again around one o'clock.

"It's certainly different from my last job when I was up at six and often working through until nine-thirty at night."

With Paul having had such a 'glamorous' job before starting out on his football career, there was no way he was going to escape a barrage of mickey-taking from his new team-mates.

"The lads here do give me a fair bit of stick about what I used to do," he continues. "For example, each time I step forward to take a penalty in training they start making mobile phone noises. I have to admit, though, I did have a mobile!

"On first arriving I heard that people were saying I took a big pay cut to join United, that I earned more in the City than I was doing at Bramall Lane. I have to say that isn't true. I'm on more money here than I was in London.

"The move originally came very much out of the blue for me. I hadn't any idea Sheffield United manager Dave Bassett was interested. As far as I was aware, the only club who had made an approach were Fourth Division Barnet, but at the time Sutton wouldn't let me go.

"But to move straight from non-League to the First Division really was a dream. But I wasted no time making sure it wasn't a short-lived one. I was aware that it's all very well winning a place in the side and playing a few games, but I also knew I had to produce the goods every week to keep my place in the team.

"At first I went out on to the pitch just determined to enjoy myself and was quite pleased with the way things went. The fact that United play a similar system to the one I was used to at Sutton helped.

"It also helped that a lot of the lads here are Southerners, like myself. While I didn't know much about Sheffield United as a club before I arrived, I did know all about a few of the players from the time they spent with clubs down south.

"That was important in my settling down here and that always helps your form on the field."

CHARLIE NICHOLAS
CELTIC

44

KEEP BACK — IT'S MY BALL!

Spurs' PAUL STEWART bars all roads to SCOT GEMMILL (Nottingham Forest).

IT'S

A FOOTBALL club is like a big family. I should know because I was one of ten children myself. Being part of the Campbell clan taught me plenty about life and sport. We were always playing games involving all the kids.

Eighth of the ten children but youngest of the five boys, I was lucky enough to get greater opportunities coming my way. Several of my family were very good at sport. My brothers Errol and Patrick could both have played professional football with a bit of luck, and the girls were quite good at the game too.

It wasn't just football we played. We'd try our hand at anything and I particularly enjoyed swimming and running at school.

But football was always my favourite game and my ambition was to be a professional. I was lucky enough to train with several of the clubs in London, including West Ham, Charlton and Chelsea.

Then, when I was 13, I made the decision to follow my school-friend Michael Thomas to Highbury. It didn't take me long to realise I had made the right decision — Arsenal was a great club to be part of, even as a schoolboy.

Right from the start it was a battle for all the boys to make a good impression on the coaching staff. Only a few of us would be offered apprenticeships at 16, even fewer, professional contracts at 18.

I was one of the lucky ones, being kept on at 16 and given my chance in the Arsenal Youth team. Things went very well for me at that level. I scored plenty of goals and in 1988 we reached the FA Youth Cup Final.

We played Doncaster in the two-leg final. But it was all over after the away leg when I scored a hat-trick in our 5-0 win. The second game was a formality but I still had 120 of my friends and family in the stands at Highbury.

A BATTLE!

Arsenal's KEVIN CAMPBELL faces fierce competition for a first team place.

That game took place on May 3rd, but, incredibly, the best was still to happen that season. Four days later, manager George Graham included me in the squad for the final Division One game at Everton and I came on as a late substitute.

I knew that short debut appearance didn't mean I'd made it at the age of 18. I was still a long way from becoming a first-team regular.

The boss had plans for me during the next season. He arranged for me to go on loan to Fourth Division Leyton Orient. This was to be the first part of my education on how to become a top striker.

So, in January 1989, I took the short trip across north London from Highbury to Brisbane Road. Leyton Orient were sixteenth at the time and things didn't look very promising.

But three months later, they were on their way to the play-offs, which they went on to win. I'd scored my first nine League goals and gained some valuable experience.

Arsenal were champions that year, but I'd played no part in that. But at least I'd helped Leyton Orient win promotion to Division Three. My loan period ran out before the play-offs, but I went back to join in their celebrations.

It was at Brisbane Road that I really started learning about football. The difference between reserve football and the League, even Division Four, took me by surprise.

Even after the success of my time with Leyton Orient, George Graham still thought I had some way to go before I was ready for the top flight. So, the next season, he arranged for

me to spend two months on loan with Leicester City.

That meant a step up to Division Two. But thankfully it didn't stop the goals coming. Just as important was the fact that I started developing the creative side of my game while I was at Filbert Street.

Discipline was something else I added to my game during my early League experience. I've always tried to play the game hard but fair. I've been called 'Rambo' and 'Rottweiler' at different times in my career, but that doesn't mean I'm a dirty player. I've got a good disciplinary record and I want to keep that.

This time when I returned to Highbury, the boss decided I was finally ready for a run in the first team. I played eight full games and was sub for another seven. I thought that would put me in a strong position to challenge for a regular place the next season.

Things didn't quite go according

to that plan because I got injured the day before the first match. It wasn't too serious but it still cost me a place until February. Only then did I get called in to the team that was leading the First Division.

My task was simple enough — I just had to score enough goals to stay in the team, and keep Arsenal on top of the table. Thankfully I managed to bag nine and that helped us win the championship again.

This time I was sure I had earned a regular first team place. But the next season the boss had a surprise in store when he signed Ian Wright from Crystal Palace.

That meant an incredible battle for places in the Arsenal front-line. Alan Smith, Paul Merson, Ian Wright and myself were all internationals so it was just as tough a fight as for places in the England squad. It went on all season and I could never be sure of my place.

That's life at Highbury. You can never take anything for granted. A player has to be international class to get in the team.

My own international experience has come with the England Under-21 and B squads. Now in the next two years I'm hoping to force my way in to the full squad before the 1994 World Cup in America.

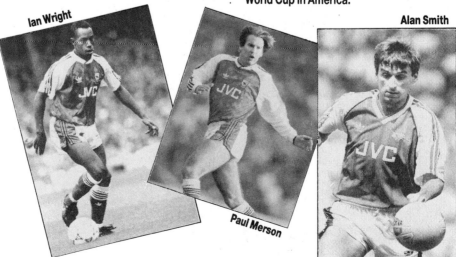

Ian Wright

Paul Merson

Alan Smith

IAN BRYSON
SHEFFIELD UNITED

STRANGLEHOLD!

Manchester City's MICHAEL VONK makes sure he keeps a tight grip on Leeds United danger man LEE CHAPMAN

I'M READY FOR ANYTHING!

WHENEVER the England football team plays a match on foreign soil, a battery of media personnel is on hand to inform the fans back home of everything that goes on within the squad.

Team news, injury worries, interviews and match reports all have to be relayed as they happen.

The Press corps attached to the international squad often outnumbers the official FA party as newspaper reporters, TV and radio commentators and photographers keep tabs on manager Graham Taylor and his players.

Consequently, the job of making everything run smoothly for the Pressmen on such trips is a major operation in itself.

That's where John Warren comes in. He is the FA's media liaison man when travelling abroad. His brief includes arranging Press conferences with Taylor and his players, checking visas, organising Press coaches to matches and training sessions, allocating stadium passes and telephones. If a media man has a problem, you can rely on John to sort it out.

Generally, he makes sure that everything runs smoothly from reporting at the airport prior to leaving England, right up to collecting your luggage after the return trip.

Compared with his first trip, however, any minor disaster can be treated as a hiccup. John will never forget the England B team's match in Algeria when just about every possible calamity unfolded.

He recalls, "The match was played during the height of our winter, and I'd been looking forward to a few days in the North African sunshine as a nice break. But things started to go wrong even before we left England.

"The plan was that most of the travelling group would assemble in Luton on the Saturday evening, prior to take-off the following morning. But a heavy blanket of snow which covered most of the country caused so many travelling difficulties that the flight was postponed for 24 hours.

"During that period, Daily Telegraph reporter Colin Gibson spent 23 hours in his car, Weekly News writer Stuart Mathieson drove from Stockport to Birmingham twice before getting through and Daily Mirror photographer Albert Cooper spent six hours stranded in his car by a snowdrift on the M6. Even the England manager almost didn't catch the plane.

"Wolves' goalkeeper Mike Stowell had the dual problem of having left his boots at Molineux and being trapped in his house by the snowdrifts. In the end, he hired a tractor to clear a way through the snow.

"What impressed me at the end of all this was everybody's determination to beat the weather. Every expected member of the playing squad, FA party and Press corps was on the plane when it finally took off.

"At that point, I thought it would be plain sailing. When we left Luton, we were told the temperature in Algiers was a balmy 60 degrees. I'd even taken my summer clothes.

Graham Taylor

"In fact it was only 37 degrees and we arrived in the middle of an electric storm. The lashing rain which greeted us hardly abated during our entire stay.

"On the first evening, the players left for a training session at the stadium while manager Graham Taylor gave a Press conference at the hotel.

"Half an hour later, he and assistant boss Lawrie McMenemy were taken to the session in a car. The storm was so fierce that, as it pulled away from the hotel, the

So says
JOHN WARREN
after a testing
start to his role
as FA media
liaison
officer.

indscreen wipers were blown away. The chauffeur
ove all the way with his window wound down and his
ad stuck out in order to see where he was going.

"Later still, I took a coachload of photographers to the
aining session. We arrived to find the stadium in
rkness and no sign of the team or the manager.

"While our driver had taken a short cut through a maze
backstreets, the other two vehicles were stuck in a
affic jam for an hour.

"On the night of the match, we had more lightning and
rrential rain. The huge Olympic stadium appeared
npty with only 1000 spectators inside. Wherever you
oked, floods of rainwater poured through the seams
tween each concrete section.

"Lightning hit the stadium's generator, causing a
wer cut and putting the floodlights out for 15 minutes
fore the match. They went off again for a few more
nutes during the game.

"Meanwhile, the pitch was like a swimming pool.
ayers splashed around in atrocious conditions.

"And after all that, the match finished 0-0 and Neil
ebb was sent off.

"But our problems weren't over. After a delayed
e-off, one of the journalists fell ill with suspected food
isoning during the flight and needed the attention of
e team doctor.

"On arrival at Luton, we found the airport in the grip of a
power cut. With no lights on and the conveyer belts out of
action, everybody had to grope around in the darkened
luggage hall for their cases."

After that experience, most trips are a dawdle for John,
who spent 26 years in the police force before becoming
so closely involved with football.

After a brief spell as assistant to Glen Kirton in the FA's
Press office, he left to become the Football in the
Community officer at Fulham.

Now operating as a freelance, he performs the same
role for Brentford, and also organises the Family Stand at
Wembley for England matches.

"Having also been Press officer to the British team in
the Olympics and Commonwealth Games, the FA felt my
experience could help in organising the media on
England trips," he adds.

"I felt I was being tested out on that first occasion,
though. After telling people on the Saturday night, "I'll see
you at the airport in the morning," I seemed to spend the
next few days making new arrangements to cater for
each fresh calamity.

"In a way, I was glad of it. It gave me a good insight into
what was required in the job and useful experience of
what might go wrong. I now feel I'm prepared for
anything."

left boot, then left glove...

... and that's just the start of the pre-match ritual for Oldham's JON HALLWORTH.

WHEREAS most goalkeepers just keep their fingers crossed that they won't concede a goal during a game, there are others who take rather more serious precautions.

Oldham Athletic 'keeper Jon Hallworth, for example, is arguably the most superstitious player in the game today. While many professionals have one pre-match ritual to which they attach real importance, 26-year-old former Ipswich Town man Jon has a whole collection.

In fact, at the last count there were five definite procedures Jon MUST go through before every game.

"I just wouldn't feel right if I didn't do these special things before each game," Jon explains. "There isn't a particular reason for doing any of them, I've just picked them up through my career.

"The superstitions I have are to always put my left boot and my left glove on first, to put my shirt on last and, just before we go out, to make sure I shake each team-mate by the hand before leaving the dressing-room.

"Once I get out onto the pitch I always have to kick the ball into the back of the net. I try to get as close to the goal as possible so there's virtually no chance of missing. I know that if I miss the goal then I'm bound to have a shocker.

"That once happened to me. I ran out to warm up, struck the ball at the goal and missed! I really did have a terrible match that day.

"I also make sure I never get a haircut the day before a game. Don't ask me why! It's not as if I went to the barbers one time and then had a nightmare on the pitch. It's just one of those things that I've picked up

"These days it's more habit than superstition. I feel I have to do all the things. If I didn't I'd definitely feel as though I was missing something.

"I think goalkeepers are probably the most superstitious of players. I always remember being told about former Manchester City goalkeeper Joe Corrigan. Like me, he always insisted on shaking hands with all his team-mates before matches.

"If he missed anyone out then he would get someone to unstrap his gloves so he could wish them luck. The old style gloves didn't have velcro fasteners like they do today and it was quite a job taping and tying them up.

"After Joe had shaken their hand he would have to get his gloves put back on again.

But having so many rituals on the pitch, what is Jon like off it?

"I'm not really that superstitious," he closes. "I won't walk under ladders but that's about as far as it goes. The rest is saved for match days!"

ROB
NEWMAN
NORWICH CITY

bergerac of stamford

that's Chelsea's GRAEME LE SAUX

BECOMING a professional footballer isn't easy when you come from a place like Jersey in the Channel Islands. They are only off the coast of France but they might as well be on the other side of the world as far as English football clubs are concerned.

Very few scouts go to see the youngsters on Jersey and Guernsey. That's a shame because there are plenty of promising players around. There is a lot of money in Jersey, so the facilities available for sport are brilliant. There are also some excellent coaches.

Most football clubs in England don't realise how well organised the game is on Jersey. So they just don't bother to go over and have a look round. That means that most of the kids get disheartened and don't progress in the game. They know they don't have much likelihood of being spotted.

The only way to improve your chances is to come to England as I did. And Southampton was my first port of call.

I came over while I was still at school to attend one of their summer training camps. It gave me a chance to train with some top professional coaches.

Southampton were obviously hoping to pick up some youngsters to sign on as apprentices. When

they asked me to stay on for an extra week, I realised they were interested in me. But at that stage I wasn't ready to commit myself to a career in football. I wanted to complete my education first. At the time I thought that 'A' levels were going to be very important to me.

Putting my education first seemed to put Southampton off. That didn't worry me too much because I already had my mind set on joining Chelsea instead.

The Chelsea manager at the time was John Hollins. He was very happy to wait for me to complete my education before I joined Chelsea. In fact, the learning bug didn't disappear even after I'd arrived at Stamford Bridge. It wasn't

long before I decided to take a diploma in Environmental Studies.

I've always been interested in the care of the environment and doing a course seemed to be the best way of learning all about it. In the end, I didn't last too long on the course because I was starting to make rapid progress in my football career. Once I got in to the first team, it was impossible to do the studying.

In the end it was best for everybody that I gave up on my studies. I was just getting frustrated about the situation. However, packing up the course didn't mean I forgot my interest in the subject.

Even now I don't miss a chance to tell my Chelsea team-mates what they should be doing to help. I try to encourage them to buy all the environmentally-safe products. If everybody could just do simple things like putting rubbish in the bin it would help.

Our central defender Ken Monkou and myself also got involved in a project to clear up an area of land near our training ground. That was just one example of how people could help out.

Of course, as a professional, my first priority has to be playing football. Chelsea must come first. I made my League debut for Chelsea on Boxing Day 1989 when I came on as a sub against Crystal Palace. It was a very dramatic debut as well.

We were on our way to losing the game when I scored an equaliser with seconds to go. There couldn't have been a better way to start my Chelsea career.

The next day the headlines in the newspapers were all about 'Bergerac'. It didn't surprise me to be nick-named after the TV Jersey detective and the tag's stuck.

I'm just glad to show people that there are other good things to come out of my home island besides the BBC programme. Now it's finished for good, I hope to be the best known Jersey-man of all.

Coming from the Channel Islands, I soon found I had a decision to make about my international future. Because I held a British passport, I could have played for any of the four home nations — England, Wales, Scotland or Northern Ireland.

In fact, the choice didn't end there. My name gives away the fact that I have French ancestry and it was enough to qualify me to play for France.

I like France and we often went on holiday there when I was a kid. I can even speak the language a little bit.

But, I decided eventually I didn't want to commit myself to playing for them at international level when I was playing my League football in England.

In fact, Wales were the first to show an interest in me. Terry Yorath was keen to include me in one of his squads but by that time I'd decided I wanted to represent England.

I had to wait only until the end of the season to achieve that ambition. I was selected to go on the England Under-21 trip to Toulon in France.

I played four games in the left-back position during the tournament. But I knew that wasn't going to be my regular position at Chelsea because Tony Dorigo was the number three at the time.

The chance to attack

I've always considered myself a versatile player and I feel comfortable playing in several different positions down the left-side. I've turned out at left-back, left-side midfield and as a left-winger. It doesn't really bother me as long as I get the chance to attack during a game.

I think it was probably my versatility that brought me to Graham Taylor's attention last season when he included me in the England B squad. I'd like to think I provide a few options for any manager.

You've got to take your chances when they come at international level. That's why I didn't let a bump on the head stop me travelling to Spain for a B game last season.

The incident happened during a live TV game we played against Manchester United the day before I was due to fly out to Spain. I clashed heads with United defender Paul Parker and for a minute or two I didn't know what was happening. It was quite frightening at the time because I'd never suffered a head injury before.

I felt faint and I was suffering from double-vision. Thankfully, it wasn't too long before the half-time whistle went and I had the chance to recover.

I soon dismissed any doubts that I might have to withdraw from the England squad. I would have travelled with a broken arm — let alone a little bump on the head!

STEVE
STAUNTON
ASTON VILLA

ROY
KEANE
**NOTTINGHAM
FOREST**

57

SAFETY FIRST!

That's the aim of the police moving into action at a big match.

IT'S the day of another big match at Villa Park in Birmingham, and the fans of Aston Villa and Chelsea awake looking forward to being entertained and wondering what scoreline is in store for their team.

But for another group of people the match scoreline is far from their thoughts. For West Midlands Police their goal is to ensure that spectators can attend the match without a threat to their safety.

For 99% of fans it's a fun day out, but that remaining 1% can spoil it for everyone else. With the memory of recent disasters at football grounds around Britain and the rest of Europe still fresh in our minds, the police fulfil a vital role at football matches.

We followed the West Midlands Police force through their duties at last season's First Division match between Aston Villa and Chelsea and discovered that there is a lot more to policing a football match than meets the eye of ordinary fans.

10 a.m. — Traffic cones are laid down in roads immediately outside Villa Park. They will prevent cars parking and blocking areas which will, in a few hours, become congested with traffic and thousands of fans.

12.45 p.m. — Briefing in the Police Parade Room behind the Witton End stand at Villa Park.

This is carried out by the Match Day Inspector, Inside Ground Inspector and Inside Ground Commander and is attended by about forty constables, eight sergeants, four inspectors and chief inspectors and two superintendents.

The briefing has five main objectives:

1. To ensure the safety of all fans before, during and after the game.
2. To ensure the safety of all players and officials.
3. To arrange segregation of all fans to reduce incidents of violence or anti-social behaviour. This to be carried out with courtesy and respect from all police officers.
4. To detail the action to be taken if any major incidents occur.
5. To make sure the local population are not unnecessarily inconvenienced.

In addition, information on 'away' fans and how many are expected to attend the match is passed on. Officers are also given the names of fans with bad reputations and two officers are outlined to deal with emergency evacuation procedures if they should arise.

The Villa Park ground is split into four for police purposes. They are named the Red, Green, Blue and Yellow sectors. An inspector is put in charge of each sector and ensures such things as the correct deployment of officers in his area and a proper liaison with stewards.

The whole operation will be monitored from the Police Control Room which is situated between the Trinity Road Stand and the Holte End terrace. It overlooks the pitch.

It's like the cockpit of an aeroplane with monitors, switches and levers strategically placed around the room.

There are ten monitors: Six cover the Villa Park surrounds including car parks, and four watch inside the ground. Many

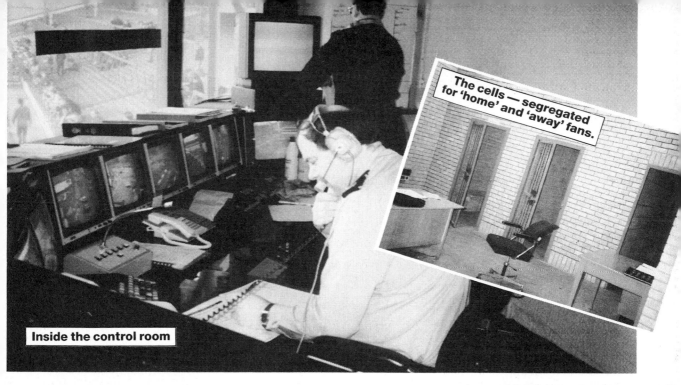

The cells — segregated for 'home' and 'away' fans.

Inside the control room

of the monitors are black and white, but most of those inside the ground are used for surveillance purposes and can focus in on a subject in great detail. These monitors are in colour.

There is also another monitor which is linked to all the turnstiles and keeps track of the attendance in all sectors of the ground. Police can find out at a glance how many people are going through the turnstiles per minute, and how long it will take at that rate for the area to reach capacity. Even the executive boxes are checked in this way.

There is an emergency public address over-ride which means that police messages can be transmitted through all tannoy systems in the ground in the event of an emergency.

1.30 p.m. — All entrances to the ground are now open.

1.31 p.m. — The first fans trickle through the turnstiles where they can be searched by club safety stewards who are looking for prohibited articles such as glasses, bottles, cans, gas canisters, fireworks, tools, knives, golf umbrellas, cameras and flag poles. Searches are done on a random basis. Police officers are not used to make searches but will be called in if an arrest is required. Fans are then shown to their seats by general stewards.

2.00 p.m. — A Traffic Exclusion Zone is put into operation in some areas around the ground. Only local residents with permits are allowed into the zone.

The police operation outside the ground is co-ordinated with the support of the dog branch, mounted branch and the operation support unit of West Midlands Police.

Visiting fans who made the journey to Birmingham by train are met at Aston and Witton railway stations by police and escorted to nearby Villa Park.

2.15 p.m. — Although the number of arrests at matches has steadily fallen over the past few seasons, there are still too many people who get into trouble.

A fan, arrested inside the ground, is taken down to the Detention Room which is situated at the rear of the North Stand. There he is handed to the custody sergeant who has to be satisfied an offence has been committed. The person will then be put into one of two temporary cell blocks which are segregated for 'home' and 'away' fans.

He will not be held in the temporary cells for more than an hour before being transferred to Queens Road Police Station. Here he is processed and documented and summonsed to appear in court. Dates for court

appearances are staggered to ensure rival fans don't clash at court.

2.50 p.m. — The Ground Inspector gives the referee instructions on what to do in the event of an emergency.

3.00 p.m. — Kick-off. Most fans should now be inside the ground. Police begin to assemble at four 'pens' situated at each corner of the ground. They are not obstructing the view from the stands but are well placed to act if there is any trouble.

4.35 p.m. — The game is nearing its end. Police and stewards begin to line the track around the pitch to prevent fans getting on the pitch at full-time.

4.40 p.m. — The final whistle goes and the crowd begins to flood out through the exits. The police who were in the 'pens' move back outside the ground.

5.00 p.m. — The only people left inside the ground are groundsmen.

5.10 p.m. — The coaches carrying visiting fans are released and given a police escort to the motorway.

5.15 p.m. — The Exclusion Zone is lifted and traffic cones are picked up. The Police Control Room is closed.

Another successful police operation at Villa Park is over.

MARK HATELEY

RANGERS

JOHN FASHANU doesn't claim to be the most skilful footballer in the game. But he is certainly the busiest — and that's very much how he likes it.

Football is only one part of the Fashanu lifestyle. He is also a businessman, television presenter, football commentator and analyst, and charity worker. Not to mention being a media 'personality' who often pops up on chat-shows, sporting occasions, social gatherings and the like.

"I'm a workaholic," confesses Fashanu. "Only really happy when I'm busy doing things. I enjoy working. But nothing will get in the way of football. First and foremost, I am a professional footballer. I have ambitions in the game.

"Although I'm involved in doing a lot of TV, and I have several business interests, nobody should get the idea that I'm moving away from football. I just enjoy keeping busy, and filling my days.

"I believe that having plenty of interests outside the game keeps me mentally fresh for football. The game is not always on my mind.

"When I report for training I am eager for it. If I just had football to think about, I would probably get stale."

NEVER A DULL MOMENT
— that's life for Wimbledon's JOHN FASHANU

Fash earned himself a big reputation last year with his BBC Television series 'Good Sport'. He was co-presenter along with actress and model Paula Hamilton.

The magazine-style programme earned good reviews, while Fashanu won praise for his relaxed, but informed approach. He is keen to do further TV work.

"Television adds another string to my bow. Doing the series was great," he says. "I enjoyed it very much, and appreciated the favourable reviews. It was a challenge, and I'd like to do more in that field."

You don't find John Fashanu hanging around after training, neither in the bar, the snooker hall nor the golf course. As soon as he has showered and changed, Fash is on the way to his offices in North London.

He has an interest in four different companies, dealing in property development, sports clothing, fashion, and promotion work. He has close ties with his native Nigeria, doing radio and TV work, as well as exporting sportswear.

Ever since he began making money as a professional footballer, Fash has put it to good use outside the game. He is intelligent and shrewd, as well as very hard-working.

Perhaps it was the time that John and big brother Justin spent in a Dr Barnardos home as youngsters, that created his desire to be a success, a 'somebody'. He is certainly successful, rumoured to be a millionaire, and has two England caps to prove his ability on the field.

John is disappointed that he hasn't added to those two England appearances in the last couple of years. Three years in succession he has scored twenty goals for Wimbledon — one of the most consistent records in the First Division.

"I was a little bit disappointed not to be selected last season, or the year before," admits Fashanu. "Two years ago I was second only to Alan Smith in the First Division scorers.

"More than that, I have sorted out my disciplinary record in the last couple of years. I rarely get booked nowadays.

"I don't know what more I have to do to get selected for the England squad. I guess I have to keep plugging away, and hope to get picked again.

"Business gives me a lot of satisfaction, but football still provides the real excitement in my life.

"I feel my game has developed in the last few years. People tend to think of me as a big bustling striker, who is good only in the air. But there is more to me than that.

"I think a breakdown of my goals proves it. I score more with my feet than with my head. I don't think I am just a target man.

"Last season the highlight for me, apart from my goals, was signing a new improved contract at Wimbledon. That gives me security for the future.

"At one time we were struggling to stay up, but once Joe Kinnear took over as manager we did very well, and clinched our place in the Premier League.

"To be up there speaks volumes for the club. I am pleased to have been a part of it. People have been writing us off for years, but we are still up with the big boys.

"It was always said that we beat teams at home because our small ground at Plough Lane intimidated the visitors. But we don't need to intimidate people to win matches.

"Certainly there was a good atmosphere at Plough Lane when it was full. But people forget we didn't actually have a great home record there in the last year or two. Our away record was almost as good.

"I don't think the ground played any part in our success. We won matches because we were a good side.

"Wimbledon is a big club and we wanted a big ground to play in. That's why we moved to Selhurst Park. It's a first-class stadium. This season I think we can prove we have a first-class team to go with it."

WEMBLEY HOO
STRUCK AGAIN

but Sunderland's PAUL BRACEWEI

SUNDERLAND captain Paul Bracewell signed off last term at the venue where every player dreams of ending his season — at Wembley.

But the Roker Park club's 2-0 defeat by Liverpool in the FA Cup Final meant that the former England internationalist's Wembley hoodoo continues.

It was the 30-year-old's fourth final, but he has yet to finish on the winning side.

Bracewell had skippered his team at Wembley, hoping to wipe out a run which had threatened to label him a perpetual FA Cup Final loser.

He says, "I was in the Everton team which reached three finals during the 1980's, but ended up on the losing side each time. Liverpool beat us twice — in 1986 and '89. Manchester United were the winners in 1985."

Despite his disappointment at failing to end that run in last season's final, ironically against Liverpool again, he has regarded his last two Wembley appearances as bonuses.

For Bracewell acknowledges that his career has been resurrected after it seemed to be all over at the age of 24. An ankle injury which virtually wiped out two years of competitive action also threatened to consign him to the soccer scrapheap.

Had that happened, that 1986 Final would have been his final professional appearance. By the time the next League season kicked off, the midfield battler was already on the sidelines fighting the injury which was to baffle the medical experts.

Only his own refusal to admit defeat, coupled with Everton's readiness to find a cure whatever the cost, enabled him to finally beat the injury.

Paul had arrived at Goodison Park in a £425,000 transfer from Sunderland in 1984, and went on to win First Division Championship and European Cup Winners' Cup medals, along with three full England caps before being struck down.

He recalls, "I went from one hospital to another and saw various specialists during an agonising 18-month spell.

"I had X-rays and scans. I listened to different opinions about what the problem might be, but came no nearer to finding the answer.

"During that spell, I also had five operations which failed to resolve the injury, and was twice told that I wouldn't play football again.

"I went through periods when I felt very low. And during the worst of those I had to prepare myself for the possibility that those verdicts were true, and that my career was really over. But I never gave up hope.

"Fortunately, Everton stood by me through every step of my ordeal. All they wanted was to save my career — for my sake.

"After I'd been told for the second time that the injury would force my retirement, they decided that, since my career was clearly on the line, they would find the top man in the world to try to save it.

"They traced a surgeon in San Francisco and arranged for me to see him. Within two days, I was on a flight to the United States.

"During that flight, the reality of my situation hit me hard. It was a nerve-wracking visit which lay ahead.

"I'd been up every other alley in the hope of finding a cure. This was to be the final throw of the dice. If it didn't come in my favour, I would have to finally accept that my career was over.

"My entire first three days in San Francisco were spent undergoing scans. It was a much more thorough process than anything I'd experienced at home. Thankfully, it proved worthwhile by finally pinpointing the problem.

"It was discovered a fragment of bone had chipped off my main ankle bone. The specialist told me that it had probably come loose after the original tackle, and had been floating around the joint ever since, somehow eluding all the previous exploratory tests.

"Having found the cause of the problem, he operated to remove the piece of bone. After that, I spent six weeks in plaster, a further six weeks building up my muscles, and finally I was ready to start battling for a first team place."

Unfortunately for Bracewell, that was not to happen. Despite a few brief runs, including his inclusion in the Everton side for the 1989 FA Cup Final, he couldn't establish himself as a regular in the Goodison Park line-up.

"I made 18 first-team appearances during the latter half of the 1988-89 season," he recalls. "But I was never able to string very many together.

OOO
. . .
s still smiling.

"When the new League programme kicked off in August '89, I was left out again. I had to assess my situation. With 18 senior players competing for places, and being quite far down that list, I felt my chances were limited.

"Reluctantly, I decided my future lay away from Everton. But I left Goodison with no grudges. Quite the opposite. They'd stood by me when I was most in need, and without the club's help I probably wouldn't be playing now."

Bracewell is also grateful to Sunderland for buying him back for £250,000 in September 1989 and giving him another chance.

"In my own mind, it was never a make-or-break season," he goes on.

"As far as I was concerned, my ankle problems were behind me and I had no fears of recurrence. I also had faith in my ability to recapture my old form.

"But I recognised that Denis Smith, who was manager of Sunderland at the time, was taking a big gamble. Though he bought me after an initial loan period, I hadn't proved my fitness conclusively.

"I owe him a lot for showing faith in me. But, considering I've put in three full years of first-team action since then, I think I've shown that the initial gamble was worth taking.

"My only regret about my lost years has been over the international career which I may have had if I'd remained free from injury.

"At the time of my ankle trouble, I'd been capped three times by England and was confident of going on to play regularly for my country. Being unavailable for so long took that chance away, and if I dwell on it for too long it depresses me to think what I might have missed.

"So I don't think too much about it. I've had other things to look forward to since coming back to Sunderland. Most of all, the excitement of last season's cup run even if it did end in disappointment.

"I'll never forget that, after being on the brink of ending my career through injury, I was given a second chance. All I've ever tried to do for the past three years — and will continue to do — is make the most of that good fortune."

A Surprise Packed Season!

for Spurs' ANDY GRAY

IT was a game England couldn't afford to lose. Graham Taylor's reputation as an international manager was on the line.

The venue was Poznan, the opponents Poland, and the occasion was England's final European Championship qualifying game on November 13th, 1991.

A draw would see Taylor's men through to the finals in Sweden. Defeat would have meant Jack Charlton's Eire team taking that place.

For such an important game, Taylor was expected to choose his most experienced line-up. But he had other ideas.

The England manager decided to take a gamble by giving full England debuts to Andy Sinton and Andy Gray. It was a risk that almost back-fired badly on Taylor.

Gray, like many before him, appeared to freeze on the big occasion. When presented with a clear-cut chance in front of goal, he blasted the ball badly wide.

Not surprisingly, he was substituted at half-time with England 1-0 down. Fortunately, Gary Lineker scored a vital equaliser in the second-half and England were on their way to Sweden.

But Andy Gray soon realised he wouldn't be amongst those going to the European Championship. Even now he doesn't understand why he wasn't given a second chance.

"I still don't know what I did wrong that night in Poland," says Andy. "Did I really play that badly?

"My international debut had been a long time coming. I was 27 by the time I pulled on an England shirt for the first time at full level.

"Then it was all over very quickly. The first-half, during which I had that one good chance, flew past and at half-time it was all over for me. Graham Taylor decided he needed to switch things around and I was the one to be substituted as a result of that change of plan.

"After that I didn't get another sniff of international football last season. It was very disappointing but I'm hopeful that as a Spurs' player more chances will come my way.

"Joining Tottenham was just one of the many surprising things that happened to me last season. At the start of the campaign I was just hoping for a settled year with Crystal Palace and to at least establish my international career. But it didn't quite work out like that.

"I was in my second spell at Palace after brief periods with Aston Villa and QPR. I was looking forward to helping the team build on the success of the previous two years. During that time we had reached the FA Cup Final, won the Zenith Data Systems Cup and finished third in the League."

The start of last season spelt trouble for Crystal Palace. Controversy seemed to follow Steve Coppell's team wherever they went.

Early problems arose after chairman Ron Noades made some rather provocative remarks about black players on a TV documentary. It caused quite a stir but Andy helped to calm things down by publicly supporting his chairman.

But soon after that, Palace sold their star-player Ian Wright to Arsenal. They were paid £2.5 million for him but Coppell spent the rest of the season trying to sort out a suitable replacement.

Then, with his England disappointments clearly a factor, Andy Gray fell out badly with Steve Coppell over his attitude to training. It was soon clear he would have to move to re-launch his career once more.

Tottenham quickly sorted out a deal that would take Andy to White Hart Lane on loan for three months, before a £750,000 move was completed.

The only problem was that his move coincided with Tottenham's important Rumbelows and European Cup Winners' Cup games. He wasn't eligible to play in these matches.

"Having to sit out those games meant I was struggling for match fitness when I did play." Andy explains. "I put on a few unwanted pounds and that tended to catch up with me in the last ten minutes of a match when I got quite tired.

"It was all my own fault. In my last couple of months at Palace I'd not been very disciplined about my fitness. I paid for that when I first got to Tottenham and it was a valuable lesson to learn. I promised then that I wouldn't allow myself to get out of condition like that again.

"The manager Peter Shreeves knew all about my problems and encouraged me with my plans to put things right.

"As self-imposed punishment I vowed to do extra-training so that I would be in tip-top shape for the start of the Premier League. I knew that was the only way I was going to be of value to Spurs — and perhaps even England too."

STEVE BRUCE

MANCHESTER UNITED

SHOCK WAS

for JEREM

INTERNATIONAL recognition came as quite a shock to me. I'd never even considered the possibility of playing anything but League football.

Welsh manager Terry Yorath had other plans. He'd spotted in the records that I was born in Cyprus. That meant I could play for any of the four home countries — including Wales.

I was actually in the island for only the first six weeks of my life having been born in a British military hospital. My father was a Colour Sergeant in the Gloucestershire Regiment, who were stationed in Cyprus at the time.

My family is English and I've always considered myself English. But when it comes to playing international football, I'm now a Welshman.

I'd heard Terry Yorath was thinking about picking me for one of his squads but I quickly dismissed the idea in my own mind. After all, I was hardly established in the Norwich City first-team at the time.

But he'd decided he wanted to take a look at me at international level so I was picked for a game against Iceland. Suddenly my career had received a totally unexpected boost.

It was all very different to what I was used to at Carrow Road. Thankfully, my Norwich team-mates Mark Bowen and David Phillips had plenty of experience of life in the Welsh camp. They told me what was what and before long I was at least feeling like an honorary Welshman. Learning the national anthem took a bit longer!

I might not sound very Welsh, although I did live there for a couple of years when I was younger, but I'm very proud to turn out for my adopted country.

Thanks to Terry Yorath's sharp eye my career had taken off in a new direction. If I never play for Wales again it would still rate as a bonus.

But of course I would love to remain involved as we try to qualify for the 1994 World Cup Finals in the United States. With players like Ian Rush, Mark Hughes, Dean Saunders, Mark Pembridge and Ryan Giggs, we've got potentially a very exciting team.

Ryan Giggs is one of the most exceptional young players in football. He's got skill and pace and should do great things for Wales over the next few years. I'm glad he's on our side.

CALL-UP A BOOST...

OSS (Norwich)

TERRY YORATH

Wales did very well in the European Championships, only just missing out to Germany in the group. This time we've got a great chance to get to a major finals at last.

Ironically, when the draw was made for the World Cup qualifying campaign, Cyprus were drawn in the same group as us. Everyone else would have been looking at the names of the top teams, Romania, Belgium and Czechoslovakia but I was more interested in Cyprus. I'd always wanted to go back and see the place where I was born.

Another place I'm desperate to see is Wembley stadium. After losing in the FA Cup semi-finals last season, I can't wait for another chance to get there.

That game against Sunderland at Hillsborough was a total let-down for us. Beforehand, everything had seemed right and Norwich looked set to reach an FA Cup Final for the first time.

Our preparation was good and the atmosphere at the ground was terrific. The fans were making a great noise and there were balloons everywhere.

Up until then I'd had my best ever season at the club. I'd played more first-team games than before and was confident about helping Norwich get to Wembley.

Sadly, everything went badly wrong. Too many of our players had off days, including I have to admit, myself. After Sunderland went ahead in the first half, we just couldn't find a way back in to the game. They were only a Second Division team but we could find no way past them.

It was a devastating experience. Friends and family, and even Sunderland fans, tried to console us after the match but we all felt terrible.

I just don't know what happened. Perhaps the occasion just got to our nerves. We certainly didn't play like we knew we were capable of and I was just as guilty as anybody else. I had no interest in the Final after that — it didn't matter to me anymore.

That result was to have serious consequences when we had to return to League football. The season seemed over but we soon discovered we had a relegation battle on our hands.

First we lost to Arsenal, then West Ham, and before long we were in trouble near the bottom of the table. We were looking over our shoulders and hoping other teams would keep losing. The way we were playing at the time, we probably deserved to be relegated. It's lucky we'd collected enough points in the first-half of the season.

In the end we had to get a single point from the penultimate game of the season against Wimbledon. Not opposition you would choose to fight for your life against. They didn't need the points but that didn't stop them giving us a tough time.

It was all pretty desperate but thankfully we ended the game with the precious point we needed for survival. With the Premier League kicking-off this season that was probably one of the most important points in Norwich's history.

The relief was incredible but there was still another shock in store for us last season. The day before the final game, Dave Stringer resigned as boss.

That just summed up a season that had promised so much but faded badly. I'm looking for much better this year.

CROSSWORD

ANSWERS ON PAGE 124.

CLUES ACROSS

7 & 8 A top gunner (6, 6)
10 He's quick at Elland Road (5)
11 Time after ninety minutes (5)
12 Chelsea boss, Ian .... (11)
15 Villa's big Cyrille (5)
18 Keepers need a good pair (5)
21 Short First Division side (1, 1, 1)
22 & 23 He's at home at Ewood Park (6, 6)

CLUES DOWN

1 Manchester United defender Paul (6)
2 Players often run out of these (5)
3 You need to be injury free to be an ever .... (7)
4 Every club is after this (5)
5 Small clubs often cause this in the cup (5)
6 Some tackles are this! (6)
9 They went to the wall last season (9)
13 Span the Chelsea ground (6)
14 All managers suffer this (6)
16 Some teams and players win this (5)
17 Fire at goal (5)
19 Steve's a Kop favourite (5)
20 Group of players (5)

He's the answer to 7 and 8 across.

QUICK QUIZ

1. In 1985, two Aston Villa players joined Italian club Bari for a combined fee of £750,000. One is now with Glasgow Rangers, while the other is a midfielder with Blackburn Rovers. From those clubs, can you identify them?

2. Celtic hold the record for the most number of League Cup Final victories in succession. Have they won it three, four or five times?

3. In 1991, Wrexham finished bottom of the Fourth Division, but they weren't relegated to the Vauxhall Conference. Who joined the Fourth Division to make it a 93 club Football League?

4. Which club, who won the First Division Championship three seasons running in the 1920's, play at Leeds Road?

5. Who was Rangers' hat-trick hero against Celtic in the 1983/84 League Cup Final?

6. Which country were the first to defeat England at Wembley? The year was 1953 and it was either Hungary, West Germany or Holland.

7. Which Yorkshire club, currently in the Third Division, have staged Rugby League matches at their ground. Here's a major clue . . . they play at Boothferry Park.

8. Name the Third Division club who play on an artificial pitch.

9. You're on holiday in the Mediterranean and you buy tickets for Aris Salonika against A.E.K. Which country are you in?

10. Which club from Paisley play at Love Street?

TONY DORIGO
LEEDS UNITED

LET ME DO THE

Language expert GEORGE SCANLON on his key role behind the scenes.

ONLY one person outside of Manchester United's players and management team was privy to the inside story of the highs and lows of last season at Old Trafford.

He was there at Wembley when manager Alex Ferguson delivered the pre-match plan which beat Nottingham Forest to land the Rumbelows Cup. He was in the dressing-room at Anfield as the reality of United's title loss sank in.

This man has also shared the inner-most secrets of the dressing-room with managers like Kenny Dalglish, Graeme Souness, and England

bosses Ron Greenwood, Bobby Robson and Graham Taylor . . . he can even claim to have had a hand in England's World Cup victory over West Germany in 1966!

The man in question, who is welcomed behind the closed doors of a football team's changing room and was allowed to sit through every one of Alex Ferguson's pre-match team talks last term, is Merseysider George Scanlon.

Scanlon is the man who as interpreter guided United's Ukrainian winger Andrei Kanchelskis through his first season in England.

His role as Kanchelskis'

TALKING!

mouthpiece follows on from that of interpreter for other Soviet Union stars such as Sergei Baltacha when he was at Ipswich (now St Johnstone) and Glasgow Rangers pair Oleg Kuznetsov and Alexei Mikhailichenko.

In his 25 years as interpreter for teams travelling for European competitions and friendlies to the Soviet Union — now the Commonwealth of Independent States — and more recently acting for individuals like Kanchelskis, George Scanlon has worked with most of the top managers and the biggest clubs in the country as well as international trips with England, Scotland and Wales.

Scanlon has been able to successfully marry his footballing background with his love for languages.

A former Everton schoolboy, he gave up the chance to pursue a professional career at Goodison only in order that he could continue with his studies. Even so he still managed to play at Wembley four times and score three goals there for Cambridge University in the late fifties!

"My links with Soviet soccer began in 1966 when I was a lecturer of Russian at Liverpool Polytechnic," George explains.

"I was invited to be the attaché to the Russian World Cup side that reached the semi-finals of the tournament in England.

"I was also asked to look after the Russian linesman who officiated at the final when England beat West Germany 4-2. He was the man the referee consulted when Geoff Hurst's shot hit the bar and bounced down on the line. The Russian linesman gave the goal and England went into a 3-2 lead.

"I've always said it was my hospitality which swung his decision in England's favour that day!"

After that breakthrough into football circles as an interpreter, George then virtually had the monopoly as a guide and interpreter to any club who travelled to the Soviet Union.

When Soviet stars began to filter into the English game in 1989 with Sergei Baltacha's move to Ipswich, Scanlon left Liverpool Polytechnic — where he'd risen to become the Dean of the Faculty of Humanities — to concentrate on helping the individual players in their new world.

It has led to some amusing stories like the time Baltacha phoned George with a query about his children's school uniforms.

Scanlon explains, "Sergei told me that he'd just received a letter from the headmaster of the school where his children were due to start. In the letter it stated that uniforms had to be worn. Baltacha looked up the word 'worn' in the dictionary because he didn't understand it and found out that it meant 'old and frayed'. He rang me to ask what he should do because he'd just bought them all new uniforms!

"Andrei Kanchelskis also had a similar language difficulty last season. The word for trial in the Soviet Union is Sud (pronounced 'suit'). One day I was unable to interpret for Andrei and United had to get in touch with him about an evening function.

"He was told that he had to take his suit with him. The girl at Old Trafford kept repeating the word 'suit' to get the message through to Andrei. The day prior to this he had had his radio stolen out of his car and Andrei thought the 'suit' message was about his stolen radio. He just couldn't understand why he had to go to trial because of it!

"But apart from little incidents like that his first season in England went very smoothly. I had to sit through Alex Ferguson's pre-match talks and any tactical discussions during training and translate everything that was said to Andrei.

"Having a footballing background myself — I was manager of Merseyside non-League side Marine for four years in the sixties — I was able to fully understand the messages and tactical talk Alex needed to get through."

Scanlon also had to guide Kanchelskis through the difficulties of settling in a new country.

"In the Soviet Union even the top players are on low wages. They have small club flats and drive very modest cars. Andrei came to Manchester and was in a big house with his 18-year-old wife, had a very smart car and, most unusual for him, he had the freedom of unrestricted movement.

"That sort of sudden freedom does take some getting used to. You then have the problem of furnishing the house, calling plumbers in, having carpets fitted. Easy for anyone to arrange in their own country, but not when you don't speak the language.

"I even had to explain to Andrei that the parking tickets he was getting were not autograph hunters leaving notes on his windscreen for his signature!

"Nevertheless, I think it was a season he enjoyed and one which I thoroughly enjoyed. Manchester United looked after both Andrei and myself excellently.

"Andrei Kanchelskis has class in his feet and will be around in this country for a long time."

ANDREI
KANCHELSKIS

MARK WALTON

NORWICH

JOHN EBBRELL
EVERTON

RED CARD DOUBLE WAS TURNING POINT

FOR SPURS' PAUL STEWART

PAUL STEWART'S career has taken off in the last two years. From being a struggling striker with Spurs, short of goals and confidence, he has become an international midfield player, a key figure at White Hart Lane — and all because a referee sent off two of his Spurs team-mates!

The turning point for Paul Stewart came in a match against Luton Town at White Hart Lane. It was December 22, 1990. Paul didn't know it at the time, but his football life would never be the same again.

It was a stormy match. Spurs went behind to an early goal. Stewart, playing up front, equalised. At 1-1 it was anybody's game.

But then referee David Elleray stepped in. He sent off Pat van den Hauwe for a foul, and followed up by dismissing Nayim. Reduced to nine men — and with injury affecting Paul Gascoigne — Spurs had to re-organise.

Paul Stewart dropped back into midfield — and did a magnificent job to lead the fight-back. He even found the strength to go forward and score the winning goal.

Stewart's display persuaded manager Terry Venables to give him a run in a midfield role, in particular when Gascoigne dropped out through injury.

Paul never looked back. As Spurs progressed to the F.A. Cup Final, Paul established himself in the midfield role. Scoring the equaliser against Forest, at Wembley, he ended the season in the England B team, as a midfield player.

"I never worried too much about scoring goals when I was a striker, as long as I was contributing to the side," says Stewart. "Getting fewer chances, by dropping back into midfield, never bothered me.

"I just enjoy getting stuck in, being involved in the game, whatever position I play. Playing in midfield does suit me because there is a little bit more room.

Pat Van Den Hauwe

Nayim

"I can't see myself ever playing up front again. I consider myself a midfield player now. I've really enjoyed the last year and a half.

"It took me a long time to find the position that suits me best, but I'm making the most of it. Even now, I'm still learning about the role.

"I'm discovering things about the position in every game. But the move has given me the chance to win an England cap, and now I'm looking forward to the best years of my career."

For three years after signing for Spurs, Paul Stewart was plagued by rumours of him being 'unsettled' at White Hart Lane. There were constant newspaper stories about him wanting to return to his native Lancashire.

But last season he finally ended the speculation by signing a new four year contract for Spurs.

"I don't know where all the stories came from," admits Paul. "I've been dogged by these tales for years. They seem to start appearing as soon as I joined Spurs, and I got fed up with reading them.

"Last year the rumours were fuelled by the fact that I sold my house in London, and my wife and children moved back north. But that didn't mean I wanted to leave Tottenham.

"My family felt more settled back in Blackpool, but I still manage to see them at weekends, and occasionally during the week. I was very happy to sign a new contract for Spurs.

"The manager and coach at Spurs are family men, who understand my position. They are sympathetic to my needs when necessary.

"When possible my wife and two children spend time with me in London, but my son has just started at a new school, and I didn't want to disrupt his education.

"I don't make anything of it. I wouldn't have signed for Spurs if I wasn't sure it was what I wanted.

"It took a lot of thought before I agreed to sign, only because I had to be sure it was the right deal for me. It was a crucial stage in my career.

"Signing it was a weight off my shoulders. It was great to be able to concentrate on football, which is all that I ever wanted to do."

Stewart joined Spurs at the same time as Paul Gascoigne. The two players became best pals. For three years it was Gascoigne always getting the attention, with Stewart overshadowed.

But after Gazza's knee injury, Stewart took some of the limelight — though not Gascoigne's role in the side.

"You can't possibly replace someone like Gazza. It is an honour to be spoken about in the same breath as him," admits Paul.

"I just do a job for the team that suits my style of play. Gazza is a totally different type of player. I could never try to be a replacement.

"But I'd love to play alongside him in midfield again. To do so in the England team would be a dream come true."

DAVID BATTY
LEEDS UNITED

MAKING HIS MARK!
Liverpool's MARK WRIGHT rises to the occasion to outjump KEVIN GALLAGHER (Coventry).

77

THE WRIGHT WAY

I'M delighted with the way my career has gone so far, and believe working my way up from the lower divisions to a place in the Premier League has been the correct route.

However, my career could quite easily have taken a different direction if I hadn't resisted the temptation to join two of the biggest clubs in the country.

Born and brought up in Manchester, I was playing for a Sunday League side when Blackpool invited me to sign schoolboy forms.

Before I joined Blackpool, Manchester City and Manchester United were looking at me. But I had no regrets about not waiting for them to move to sign me.

If I had joined United, I'd probably have spent years fighting to win a place in their reserve team, and wondering if I'd ever come close to being a candidate for their first team.

I enjoyed my time at Blackpool and the experience I picked up there was invaluable. I played over 100 games for the club. Most players my age would have had only a handful of first-team matches.

I was just 16 when I made my debut for Blackpool in the second last League game of season 1987-88. We beat Chesterfield 1-0. That was in the Third Division but sadly we were soon relegated to Division Four.

Although naturally the standard of football in Division Four isn't as high as in the Second, it was very much a learning experience for me. I would have been prepared to stay on at Blackpool for a while longer and learn from such players as Andy Garner.

But when I learned that Blackburn Rovers wanted to sign me in October 1991 I needed no second invitation. It was an even greater surprise for me because I had no idea that it was going to happen until almost the last minute.

I had left my Manchester home one morning and travelled up to Blackpool's training ground expecting a normal day's work.

But when I arrived, I was told not to bother changing but to go to Bloomfield Park and speak with 'Pool boss Billy Ayre. After a brief chat with him I travelled to Ewood Park.

I didn't know Kenny Dalglish was watching me. I knew he had been at our match at Burnley the previous Tuesday, but he could have been looking at any one of several players who were on the park that night.

In fact, I met up with Manchester City assistant manager Sam Ellis, after the game. Sam was the man who signed me for Blackpool when he was boss there. It seemed City were the club more likely to be showing an interest in me. However it was Blackburn who made the offer which I accepted immediately.

Although I joined a Second Division club, it felt like I was joining a First Division club in all but name. Everything was geared to winning promotion. It was exciting to know that I was very much involved in that process.

It took me only about ten minutes of my Blackburn debut against Grimsby to realise that I could only improve my performances by playing with Blackburn.

Playing for Blackpool I had very little time on the ball before I was closed down. As a result, it was often a case of whacking it upfield for the front men to chase.

In the Second Division, however a player has more time on the ball because opponents are less likely to commit themselves to a tackle. It leads to more accurate and intelligent passing.

People say I play in a style similar to Kenny Sansom, the former England left-back. It's nice to be likened to someone who's enjoyed so much success, but I think it's mainly because we are both small and play in the same position.

The left-back I admire most is Stuart Pearce of Nottingham Forest, definitely the best number three in the country.

Like Stuart, I try to get forward at every opportunity. He must also be the most powerful tackler in the Football League.

I'll admit, in terms of build, I don't look a bit like Stuart. He isn't particularly tall but is a very tough character. I'm only 5 ft. 4 ins. and weigh just nine stone.

I may be one of the smallest players in the Football League but it isn't something that bothers me.

I keep getting asked if it's a disadvantage, but you don't have to be tall to be a left-back. Anyway I think I've a good spring when I jump for the ball.

Although I'm still only 20 and have spent most of my career in Division Four, I've been fortunate

STUART PEARCE

TO THE TOP

to have played against quite a lot of foreign opposition at various age levels.

I've now been chosen for England at every stage from schoolboy to Under-21s.

I find the style of international football is vastly different to that in the Football League. Foreign players are technically better than players of a comparable age in this country, and like to spend more time on the ball.

They're also more defensive-minded, with everyone retreating to their own half when the opposition attack.

A year ago I was a member of the England squad in the World Youth Cup Finals in Portugal. I learned a lot from competing against different teams.

We were drawn in the same group as Syria, Spain and Uruguay. After losing 1-0 to Spain in our first game, we expected to beat the unknown Syrians, but discovered their technique was superior to ours. Their ball control and passing was a revelation. Only our passion and fitness earned us a 3-3 draw.

I came home realising I would have to improve my ball skills to become a top-class player.

Although the Portugese-experience was a big disappointment at the time, I believe it has stood me in good stead.

During the tournament I found myself diving into tackles much too often and then was only able to watch as the attacker dribbled past me.

With that experience under my belt, I was more prepared to cope with opponents when I moved to Blackburn. I was able to stand up to the man with the ball.

Last season I got the call up to the England U-21 squad and that was a very big jump for me. I was rubbing shoulders with class players such as Paul Warhurst of Sheffield Wednesday and Alan Shearer of Southampton.

Alan is now a recognised member of the England squad. My aim is to join up with him in the full squad in the near future.

JASON
DOZZELL
IPSWICH TOWN

DEAN
EMERSON
COVENTRY CITY

YOU CAN'T STAND

MY career has progressed so fast in the last few years. I can hardly believe that I've made it to international level, picking up my first cap for England last season.

But now I have to try to keep the momentum going, and build on what I have achieved. That's why I was happy to sign a new long-term contract with Crystal Palace last season.

Everything has happened for me since I joined Palace. I signed a new deal at Selhurst Park because I believe I can help the club become one of the best in the country and improve my own game.

Expectations at Crystal Palace have risen over the last few years. Last season there was disappointment when we were stuck in mid-table, having finished the previous season in third place.

Yet a few years ago, everyone at Selhurst Park would have jumped at the chance of that sort of position in the First Division. You can never be satisfied in football. You must always want to do better.

My own career has grown along with the club. Almost every year I've had to raise my standards.

I joined Palace from Crewe, and had to adjust quickly from Fourth Division to Second Division football. A year later I had to bridge the gap between Division Two and the First Division. Within months I found myself picked for the England B squad, and had to make another step-up.

Then came senior international football, and another jump in standard. All the time it has been progress. Each time I've reached one level, I've been able to re-adjust, and set my sights higher.

It has been tremendous to be involved in the England squad, but I've never consciously made it a target. I've done my best for the club and looked on international football as a bonus to me.

People have tried to compare my role in the England side to that of Bryan Robson's. But not me. I just go out and do my own thing.

You could say I play in a similar position, and I have the same type of style. But that's as far as it goes. I have a very long way to go before I begin to match his achievements.

In fact I don't try to match Bryan. I concentrate on my own game, and there are plenty of things I want to improve.

As soon as you stop wanting to get better, that's the time to stop playing. I want to keep making progress in all aspects of the game.

Obviously Bryan Robson is a player I admire. But I haven't been able to watch him that much. When I was a schoolboy my hero was Colin Bell, of Manchester City.

I went to Maine Road a lot, and always admired Bell. He was a great player. I liked his attitude. He never stopped running.

Colin's work-rate was tremendous. Nothing worried him. He got on with the job. That's the sort of player I'd like to be.

Although I lived in Manchester, and was a City fan, I never made the grade there as a professional. My first club was Rochdale, but even they gave me a free transfer, and I went to Crewe.

It was there I teamed up with David Platt for the first time. He'd failed to make it at Old Trafford. We both learned a lot from Crewe manager Dario Gradi.

He taught us the right way to play football. We learned good habits at Crewe that gave us a sound basis for when we moved on. David went to Villa, and I joined Palace.

It never crossed my mind that we would end up playing in the same England midfield. But the success of Rob Jones at Liverpool shows that Crewe is a good place to start a future international career.

STEVE COPPELL has also done a lot for me at Crystal Palace. He is a great manager. Steve has done so well in organising the side, and in the transfer market.

The manager has hardly made a bad signing, and has picked out a lot of players from non-League or lower division football.

When I joined the club there wasn't a single player with international experience on the books. But in the space of a few years we've had a succession of international caps.

Ian Wright, myself, John Salako, Nigel Martyn and Andy Gray, with England; Eddy McGoldrick with Eire; and Chris Coleman (Wales); we've all won

BRYAN ROBSON

our first caps with Palace.

My first call-up for England was memorable in every way. It was the 'B' game in Algeria last year. My selection came out of the blue. I never suspected I was even close to getting in.

The game was played in appalling conditions. I just put my head down and got on with the job, and that may have impressed Graham Taylor.

I think everything we have achieved at Palace has stemmed from our FA Cup run in 1990. Beating Liverpool in the semi-final, and taking Manchester United to a replay at Wembley gave everybody confidence.

Playing in the final put us in the spotlight. It gave the players a taste of life at the top, which was an incentive to get more of it.

Last season we were in the headlines for a lot of wrong reasons. It was a difficult time for the club, but I think we came forward, and built a good platform for the future. I'm looking forward to more success.

STEVE COPPELL

NEIL RUDDOCK
SOUTHAMPTON

FLYING FAIRCLOUGH!
Oldham's sharpshooter GRAEME SHARP
is left flat-footed when Leeds' defender
CHRIS FAIRCLOUGH scales the heights.

FIRST SEASON

FIRST CLASS

DWIGHT YORKE

That's the report on Aston Villa's SHAUN TEALE

L AST season could well go down as Year of the Rookie. More first-time First Division players made their mark on the big time last term than during any other year in football's recent past.

Ryan Giggs and Andrei Kanchelskis of Manchester United, Liverpool's duo of Steve McManaman and Rob Jones for example. Then there was Manchester City's Mike Sheron and Nottingham Forest starlet Scot Gemmill. All will look on season 1991-92 as the year they really made it.

The same goes for Aston Villa striker Dwight Yorke and his defensive team-mate Shaun Teale.

But while all the other names are associated with skill and no little amount of flair, you can't say that's what helped 27-year-old Teale catch the eye. Instead it was his rock solid back-four play that made him a fan favourite.

But were it not for Villa manager Ron Atkinson's decision to make Mallorca his summer holiday destination, it's possible the Liverpool-born centre-half wouldn't have been a Villa player at all as he himself explains.

"Before joining Villa I was with Third Division Bournemouth. While manager of Bournemouth Harry Redknapp had always said he didn't want to sell me, things came to a head financially and it became clear I was on my way.

"He told me that he had people interested in me and it was best for both parties that I moved on. I knew the manager had a couple of options open, but I was left just waiting to hear where I was going.

"I knew I was on my way and I also knew that I would be going to a First Division club. I had already come up with a mini list of who I might be signing for, simply through seeing my name linked with certain clubs in the newspapers.

"I thought it could be Nottingham Forest, Wimbledon or maybe Southampton, but I never even considered Villa. I had always wanted to play in the First Division and, knowing that was where I was going, I really didn't care which club it was. I certainly wasn't disappointed when I heard it was Aston Villa, though.

"Apparently Ron Atkinson and Harry Redknapp were both holidaying in Mallorca. They met up to have dinner together one evening and I came up as a topic of conversation. But while my future was being discussed on the Mediterranean I knew nothing about it. At the time I was on holiday in America.

"Despite my relatively late start in the First Division, things had happened fairly quickly. Only three years before I had been playing non-League football with Weymouth.

"But during my time in the amateur game I worked hard and always did things as a professional would, things such as looking after my fitness. I managed to fit all that in alongside my regular job as a painter and decorator.

"But when I joined a big club like Villa it helped that I had been an apprentice at Everton. Back then I used to look up at all the big name stars and was probably in awe of them.

"A lot more self-belief"

"But I knew now I couldn't afford to look at the likes of Paul McGrath and Cyrille Regis and act in the same way. The manager told me that there was a place for me in the first-team if I didn't do that.

"While I still admire my team-mates I'm no longer in awe of them. I also reckon that my attitude is better than it was in my early days at Goodison Park.

"I have a lot more self-belief now, but that doesn't mean I tried to change anything when I arrived at Villa. I did notice differences between the Third and First Divisions but didn't do anything different.

"During my first few games I couldn't believe how long you got on the ball. You had time with it at your feet whereas you would be closed down straight away lower down the Leagues.

"You certainly get more of a breather here. In my debut against Sheffield Wednesday I hadn't even broken a sweat after twenty minutes when I really thought I'd be shattered!"

ALLY McCOIST
GLASGOW RANGERS

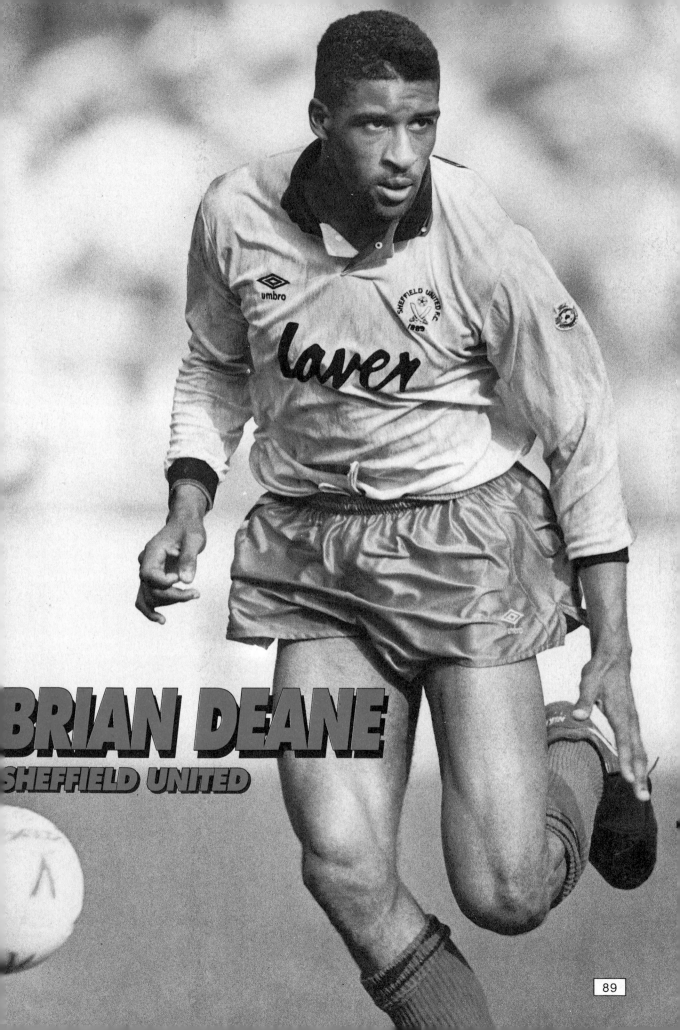

BRIAN DEANE
SHEFFIELD UNITED

MARK
WARD
EVERTON

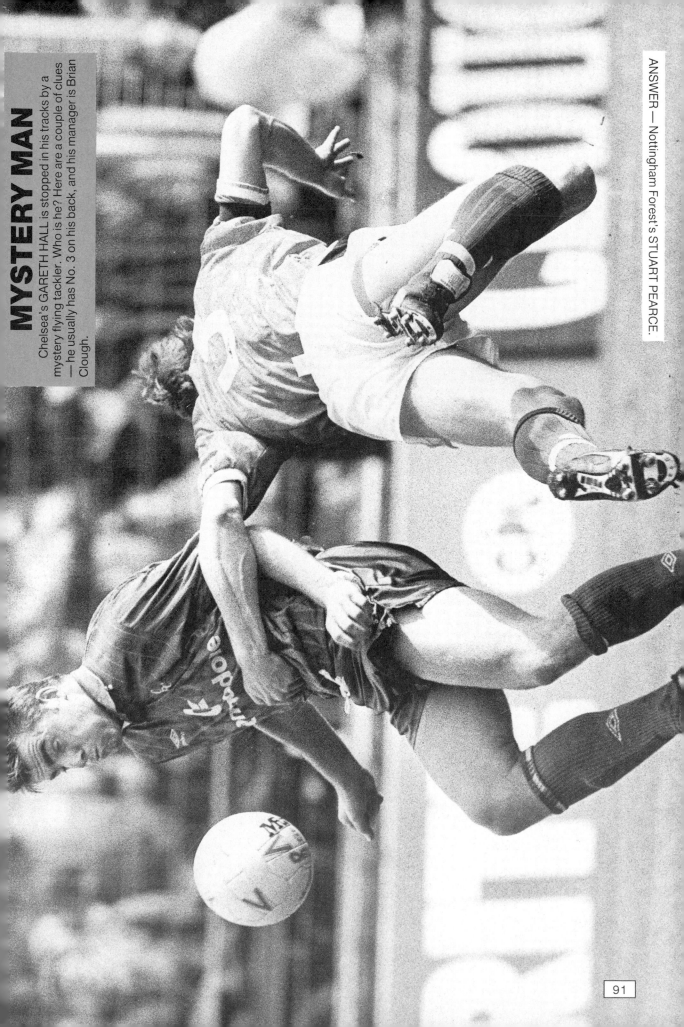

MYSTERY MAN

Chelsea's GARETH HALL is stopped in his tracks by a mystery flying tackler. Who is he? Here are a couple of clues — he usually has No. 3 on his back, and his manager is Brian Clough.

ANSWER — Nottingham Forest's STUART PEARCE.

NOTTS COUNTY manager Neil Warnock seems to believe in taking the 'Short' route in his bid to make County one of the top sides in the country.

He has been a key figure in the careers of brothers Craig and Chris Short. It's a partnership which has brought promotion to Division One and the opportunity to pit their skills against the top teams.

Warnock was manager of Fourth Division Scarborough when he introduced the brothers to the Football League, and later, when he moved to Notts County, he brought them south to link up with him again.

Craig Short explains that, although he's now rubbing shoulders with players whose photo cards he collected only a few years ago, there is no chance that he'll let the situation go to his head.

He admits that both Chris and himself have had several lucky breaks in their careers so far, including some excellent advice from important people in their lives.

Craig points out his parents have been very influential in shaping their sons' careers and, though he often doubted his own ability to be a professional footballer, his parents never did.

The defender says, "Both our parents put a lot of time and effort into helping us realise our ambition to play professional football. Any time our confidence was low and we felt like giving up, they would tell us to work hard and our hopes would come true.

"My mother is a Physical Education teacher and she would see that we ate the right foods, and encouraged us to get involved in various types of sport to build up our fitness.

"My father would drive me to training and also 'away' games. When I signed for Scarborough I didn't drive a car at the time and the buses from Pickering were very infrequent in the evenings. But even after a hard working day my father would run me to the ground for training and stay in the car and wait for me to finish."

Craig admits it was younger brother Chris who showed all the early promise of a bright future in the game.

He goes on, "Chris is two years younger than me and he has followed in my footsteps since he entered professional football. But

that wasn't always the case.

"He was the one who showed all the early promise, and while he played county football at various age levels, I didn't make the county side until I was in the sixth form at school.

"We both played for our local youth team, Pickering Town, starting in the Under-11's and going up to the Under-15's.

Notts County's CRAIG SHORT speaks his mind

"But we both thought we'd missed a career in football when as 16-year-olds we were both turned down for apprenticeships with League clubs. But the more I think about it, the less important it becomes.

"I remember playing against Middlesbrough apprentices when I was with North Riding and at least six of them are no longer in the professional game.

"But it didn't really take off for me until I joined Neil Warnock at Scarborough in 1987. They had just

joined the Football League for the first time from non-League and there was a tremendous buzz about the club. Everything was new for Scarborough and it was a great experience to be involved in the early stages of their League history.

"At that time I was playing in midfield for the reserves and didn't feel very comfortable in that position. But I can still vividly remember the turning point for me.

"We were playing against Halifax Reserves and things weren't working out for us. At half-time the boss told me to drop back to central defence. I must have made a good impression because two weeks later when the team was hit by a couple of injuries, I was thrown into the first team in my new position.

"Although I'd only been at Scarborough for just over a year, it was a great shock to me when Neil Warnock announced he was leaving to become manager of Notts County. It was New Year's Day, 1989, and we'd just beaten Crewe to climb to second in the Fourth Division. The atmosphere in the dressing-room turned from elation to gloom when the manager told us the news.

"I understand he made a bid to sign me not long after he went to County but Scarborough wouldn't

Chris Short

THE SHORT ROUTE TO SUCCESS

sell me. However, during that close season, Scarborough needed the money and were prepared to let me go. Wimbledon and Stoke showed an interest in me but I was delighted when County paid the £100,000 asking price.

"Although I knew early on that if I wanted to further my career I'd have to move from Scarborough, I was still reluctant to leave home. Going to live in a strange city always carries the risk that you may not settle there.

"However, I quickly made friends at the club and my brother Chris spent a lot of his spare time in Nottingham. He got to know several of the County players before he joined the club.

"But if Chris had got his way, he wouldn't be at County now — he'd be playing instead for Manchester United. United manager Alex Ferguson made it known he was interested in Chris and on one occasion he actually phoned my house in Nottingham to speak to my brother when he was visiting me.

"But the deal fell through and, although Chris was disappointed, he soon afterwards signed for County in July 1990 and has put that episode behind him.

"It has been great for Chris and myself to have been able to spend most of our careers so far under the management of Neil Warnock. It's also a great boost for us to know that he obviously rates us quite highly otherwise he wouldn't have brought us both from Scarborough and made us first team regulars at County.

"For all his qualities, the gaffer would be the first to admit he wasn't the best of coaches during his time at Scarborough. Mind you, he had to balance his part-time duties at 'Boro with running a chiropodist's business in Sheffield before 'Boro won promotion to the Fourth Division and he turned full-time.

"But the boss is the best motivator I've ever known and he can take a bunch of fairly ordinary players and mould them into a good team.

"He has had some good coaches with him. Colin Morris at Scarborough was one, and he currently has assistant boss Mick Jones at County. The coaches do most of the work during the week, working on our fitness, but the manager takes over on Friday and Saturday and works on the players' mental attitude.

"He has a tremendous respect for the opposition and before a match he'll take us through the strengths of all the players and explain what he wants from each of us. He places great emphasis on team work and everyone working to a 'team' plan. There are no stars in our side, just a bunch of lads who can knuckle down and get a job done.

"The boss is a bad loser and won't talk about defeat. He makes sure we never go out for a match feeling we're going to lose.

"His approach to the game is often quite different from what you'd expect. For instance, he does what I would call some really daft things, like taking us on an outward bound course and having us running along the cliffs when it's blowing a gale.

"We also have some hair-raising training routines. We have rugby matches and also a 12-a-side football match on a small pitch with fierce tackling. But all these exercises are designed to make us stronger and more determined characters and I think they succeed.

"A big advantage for County is that we have a good team spirit. It's easy for everyone to get on when the team is doing well, but when we go through a rough patch everybody sticks together and that helps us to get over it."

Craig admits it took him a while to settle in his first season in the top flight, but pitting his skills against the best players has been a great learning process for him and for brother Chris.

Under the guidance of Neil Warnock, the future looks bright for the Short brothers.

Craig Short

MEL STERLAND

LEEDS UNITED

HANDS UP!

Notts County's GEORGE PARRIS (right) and TONY DALEY (Aston Villa) cut a fancy step or two in the heat of battle.

ROLAND NILSSON

SHEFFIELD WEDNESDAY

DEAN SAUNDERS
LIVERPOOL

Ian Branfoot

GOALS

That's the aim of ALA

GOALS, goals, goals. Alan Shearer has always found a goal for the big occasion.

Whether making his League debut against Arsenal, turning out for the England under-21's, or playing for the full England team at Wembley, Shearer has never been short of a goal or two.

Like Gary Lineker, Shearer has that very special knack of finding the net when it really matters. He's definitely a big match player.

That fact was obvious from the April day back in 1988 when Alan burst on to the First Division scene at the age of seventeen. Most youngsters are very nervous when they make their League debut, but not Alan Shearer.

After just two brief appearances as substitute in away games, he ran out at the Dell for his first full League game against the mighty Arsenal. But Alan wasn't worried about the opposition — he was looking for goals.

Amazingly he came off the pitch that day with the match-ball under his arm having scored a brilliant hat-trick. The feat made him the youngest-ever scorer of a First Division hat-trick, beating Jimmy Greaves's long-standing record.

Alan might have expected to become a Saints regular after those three goals, but he had to be very patient. In fact, he had to wait well over a year before he became a first-team regular.

"My problem was that there were so many other strikers at the club at the time and I was well down the list," says Alan. "Danny and Rod Wallace, Matthew Le Tissier and Paul Rideout all made it very difficult for me to get a look-in.

"Rod and Matt quickly formed an exciting goal-scoring partnership. That made it very hard for me. They were scoring goals every week while I was stuck on the bench or in the reserves. I wondered if I would ever get in the team.

"Then, at the beginning of the 1990-91 season, everything started to move for me at last. Within a few weeks I was not only back in the Southampton team, but in the England under-21's as well.

"Lawrie McMenemy, the under-21 boss, knew all about me having been Southampton boss when I was a kid and also coming from my native north-east. I'm just glad he thought I was worth a look at for the international team."

Yet again, Alan had something special up his sleeve for his debut at international level. He scored two goals as England won away from home in Ireland.

"The international call-up gave me just the boost I needed at club level too." recalls Alan. "I wanted people to realise that I wasn't just in the Saints team as a work-horse alongside Rod and Matt.

"Graham Taylor and Lawrie McMenemy obviously thought

I was more than that. You don't get picked for England without having some ability."

Shearer's scoring record made rather interesting reading at the end of that season. He scored a total of 25 goals, only four of which came in League games.

He had clearly developed a taste for cup and international football. In domestic competitions he scored six times in the Rumbelows, twice in the FA Cup and added another two in the Zenith Data Systems Cup.

Then, during the international under-21 tournament at Toulon in France, he bagged seven more goals.

Alan was also given the honour of captaining the England team that went on to win the cup. Not surprisingly, he was named man of the tournament.

That sort of form encouraged England boss Graham Taylor to call Alan up for the England summer tour of Australia, New Zealand and Malaysia. But, he already had a previous engagement in his diary — his wedding to his girlfriend Layna.

"It was very flattering to know I was being watched by the England management," says Alan. "Although I couldn't go on that particular tour, I certainly had something to play for the next season.

"I also knew I was going to be a marked man from then on. When you start making a name for yourself as a striker, defenders pay you much closer attention.

"In the past, I'd never considered myself to be a prolific goal-scorer. But having scored all those goals for the England under-21's, I was beginning to think again.

"I even had a bet on myself to be the First Division's top scorer last season. The odds were 66-1 so I thought that had to be worth a £10 gamble.

"The season couldn't have started any better either. After just two minutes of our opening League game against Tottenham I scored with a shot from the edge of the box.

"What a perfect start to the campaign. It had to be the best goal I'd ever scored.

"I had known things were going to go well for me when manager Ian Branfoot introduced a new style of play that was directly geared to my game. Having been a provider to Matt Le Tissier and Rod Wallace, I was now being given a more important role in the Southampton team."

Almost inevitably, Alan started to be linked to nearly all the big clubs. The transfer fees mentioned rose with every game — £2 million, £3 million, £4 million! Alan Shearer was suddenly top of everybody's shopping list.

Some players would have let the big money talk worry them. But Alan has a calm head on young shoulders and found the transfer buzz inspired him to even better things.

GALORE!

SHEARER (Southampton)

"All that transfer speculation really gave my confidence a boost," explains Alan. "The sort of money being mentioned was just incredible. The important thing was not to let the situation put me off my game. With Southampton having a rather shaky start to the season in the League, the boss couldn't afford to have me dreaming up front.

"Matthew Le Tissier had also had to put up with similar transfer talk. Now it was my turn."

But Alan's main ambition was to get himself picked for the England squad. With Gary Lineker announcing his retirement from international football, Alan wanted to get to the head of the queue as his long-term replacement.

His chance finally came on February 19th, 1992. The venue was Wembley and the opposition were Michel Platini's brilliant French team.

Alan was picked to play alongside one of his rivals for Lineker's shirt — Sheffield Wednesday's David Hirst. Lineker himself started on the bench.

The first half passed fairly quietly until the final seconds were ticking away on the referee's watch. Then England won a corner.

Alan placed himself inside the six yard box, looking to pick up any chance that came his way. Neil Webb took the corner, Mark Wright rose above the French defenders to head the ball on and Alan spun neatly to volley the ball past the French 'keeper.

It was a goal Gary Lineker himself would have been proud to score. It completed a famous hat-trick of debut goals for Alan — at League, under-21 and full England levels.

In the second half, Lineker came on to team up with England's latest goal-scoring find — and Alan helped set him up for yet another international goal.

"That match was the highlight of my career," says Alan. "To score and then find myself playing alongside Gary Lineker made it quite a night."

Alan shares the goal-scoring instincts of Gary Lineker but in many ways he is more like Welsh international striker Mark Hughes — a player he has always admired.

"I'd like to think I'm similar to Mark in style," explains Alan. "He never gives up battling during a game.

"He's the sort of player the fans love to hate. But he's got all the skill required to hold the ball up against defenders and score goals.

"Like Mark, I pick up a few bookings because I have a physical approach to the game. But I don't think either of us will be changing our style.

"I aim to keep playing the way I always have, work hard and hope the breaks come my way in my career. If I can keep scoring goals at every level I'll be more than happy."

OUCH!

The faces tell the story of the stress and strain of this duel between (left) Manchester United's PAUL PARKER and Nottingham Forest's NIGEL CLOUGH.

PHIL GEE

LEICESTER CITY

BIG PUT

Manchester City's KEITH CURLE explains why.

YOUR best mate is supposed to be there to help in your hour of need. Mine forced me to gamble with my football career — but it eventually paid off when I became the country's most expensive defender at £2.5 million.

As a 20-year-old I was playing in the Third Division for my hometown club Bristol Rovers. In their squad was my best pal Ian Holloway.

When I was forced out of the first-team for an operation on a knee injury, Ian — now with Queens Park Rangers — took my place in the Rovers team. He did so well that I couldn't get back in again!

With my way blocked I had to make a decision about my future. I took a big gamble and went on loan to Torquay United in the Fourth Division and eventually I signed for them.

Although I was going down a division into the League's basement, I looked on the move as a stepping-stone rather than a step backwards. And so it proved.

I wasn't at Plainmoor long before Terry Cooper, who'd been the manager who signed me for

MONEY TRANSFER ME UNDER THE MICROSCOPE

Steve Redmond

Bristol Rovers, paid £10,000 to take me back home to Bristol City where he'd been made boss.

The irony of that move for me was that as a 16-year-old schoolboy Bristol City had told me I wasn't good enough for professional football! They wouldn't sign me as an apprentice so I was released.

However, there I was back at Ashton Gate. And it was there that Cooper converted me to the position in which I have since made my name.

He and his assistant Clive Middlemass spent an awful lot of time helping me. They saw me as a very enthusiastic kid who could probably go places with the right breaks. I suppose I was a rough diamond who needed the edges polished.

Terry had a lot of confidence in me and predicted that I would go much higher in my career and eventually make it at a big club. He also forecast that I'd end up playing for England as a right-back.

He wasn't that far wrong, for my second match as an England B player was at right-back against France.

Although Terry should know what he was talking about — he won 20 full England caps as a left-back when he was a player at Leeds United — I still believe that if I am rated as a £2.5 million centre-half, then I must be worth only about £100,000 as a full-back!

After three more seasons at Ashton Gate I suffered another setback. I had a bad ankle injury and was out for eight and a half months. I came back too soon and returned to action when I was still limping. I had lost an awful lot of my pace. There were doubts about whether I would recover all my speed.

Because of that, when Reading came in with an offer, Bristol City accepted it. I thought they were a bit hasty. But it didn't affect my career and I was soon as pacey as I ever was and I also played at Wembley with Reading when we beat First Division Luton 4-1 in the Simod Cup Final.

In 1988 I received my chance to play in the First Division when I signed for my old Bristol Rovers boss Bobby Gould at Wimbledon. My transfer fee had now gone up from £5000 to £10,000 to £150,000 and when I joined the Dons it rose to £500,000. That was an enormous gamble for them.

Wimbledon were the best club I could have joined in my path up to the top flight. I'd been used to smallish outfits and Wimbledon had no airs and graces about them, despite having established themselves in Division One.

I was able to find my feet at the top level without stepping into the goldfish bowl existence of a top club.

After three years at Plough Lane I felt ready to cope with a big club. I wanted a bigger stage to perform on. I thought Wimbledon were pricing me out of the market though at £2.5 million. It was a frightening figure and one I thought would put prospective buyers off. Fortunately, it didn't bother Manchester City boss Peter Reid.

However, I know there was a campaign of criticism aimed at myself and Steve Redmond, my City defensive partner, when I first arrived at Maine Road. Critics had a go at us for alleged deficiencies in the air.

I agree that I am not as good in the air as I should be for a centre-half. I've had people say that all my career. But I think my strengths outweigh my weaknesses. Besides I couldn't remember a header I missed throughout my debut season for City that led to a goal for our opponents.

But when you are the most expensive defender in the country you have to accept that your game will be scrutinised and criticised more than most because of the high profile you get.

That's the kind of high profile and big stage I wanted when I opted to leave Wimbledon so I cannot complain too much. Besides, overall, I don't think anyone could say Peter Reid has fallen flat on his face by paying £2,500,000 for me.

Keith Curle

LEE
CHAPMAN
LEEDS UNITED

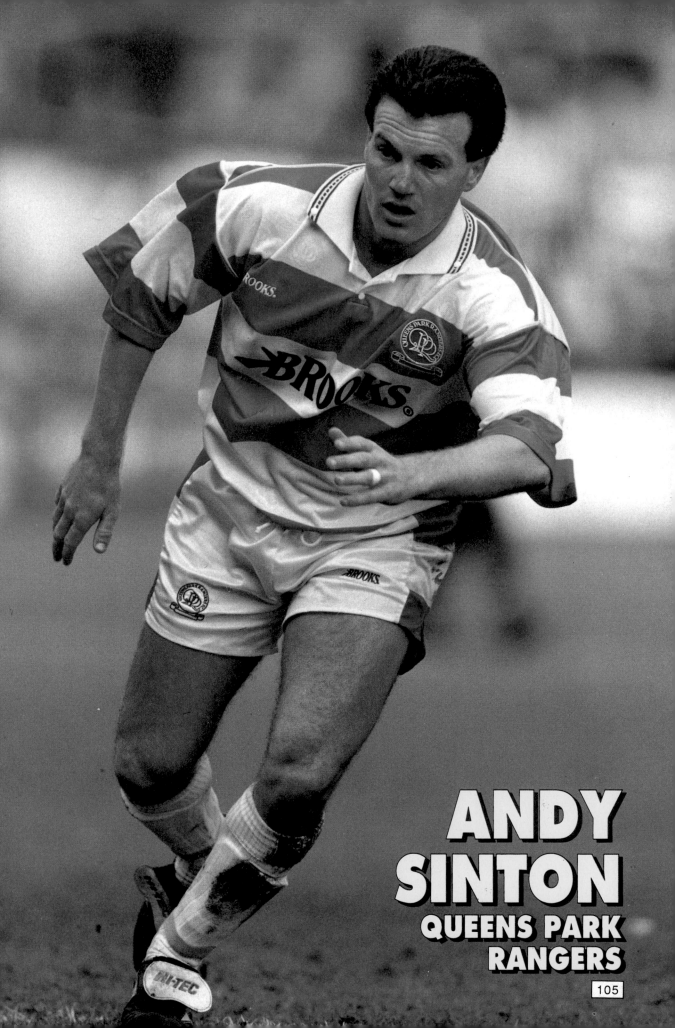

ANDY SINTON
QUEENS PARK RANGERS

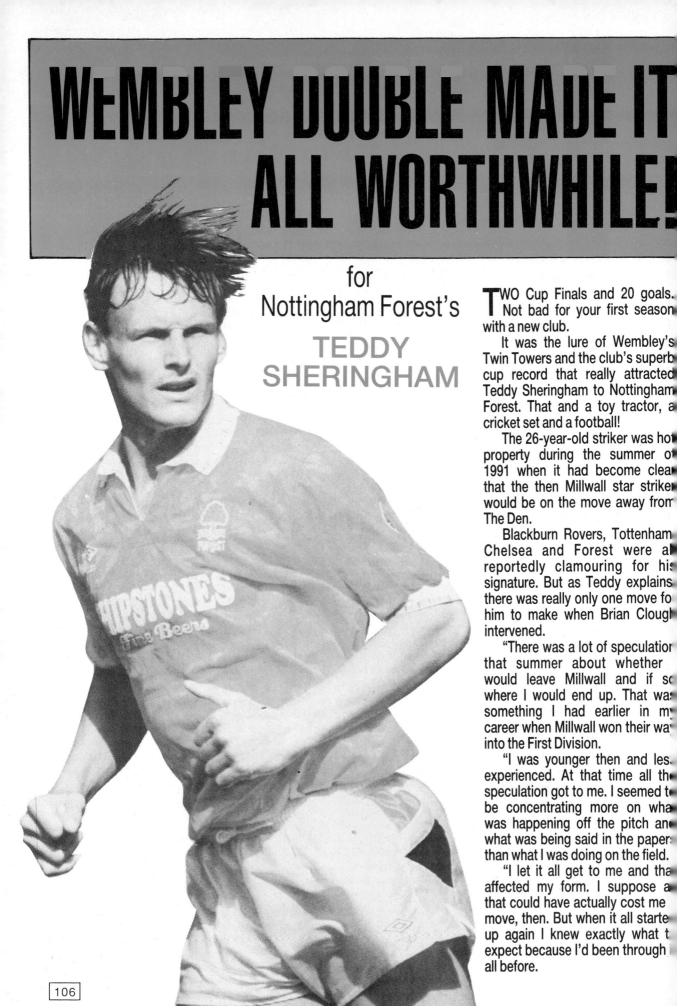

WEMBLEY DOUBLE MADE IT ALL WORTHWHILE!

for Nottingham Forest's

TEDDY SHERINGHAM

TWO Cup Finals and 20 goals. Not bad for your first season with a new club.

It was the lure of Wembley's Twin Towers and the club's superb cup record that really attracted Teddy Sheringham to Nottingham Forest. That and a toy tractor, a cricket set and a football!

The 26-year-old striker was hot property during the summer of 1991 when it had become clear that the then Millwall star striker would be on the move away from The Den.

Blackburn Rovers, Tottenham, Chelsea and Forest were all reportedly clamouring for his signature. But as Teddy explains there was really only one move for him to make when Brian Clough intervened.

"There was a lot of speculation that summer about whether I would leave Millwall and if so where I would end up. That was something I had earlier in my career when Millwall won their way into the First Division.

"I was younger then and less experienced. At that time all the speculation got to me. I seemed to be concentrating more on what was happening off the pitch and what was being said in the papers than what I was doing on the field.

"I let it all get to me and that affected my form. I suppose all that could have actually cost me a move, then. But when it all started up again I knew exactly what to expect because I'd been through it all before.

"The second time around I didn't take much notice of what the media were saying, just concentrated on my game and got on with things. My form didn't suffer and I ended up winning a move to the City Ground.

"I did speak to Blackburn Rovers but when Forest came in my decision was easy. While Blackburn were determined to make a serious bid for promotion to Division One, Forest could give me that straight away.

"I did wonder what manager Brian Clough would be like, after all, you do hear so many stories about him. But I'm not the kind of person who makes a judgment on someone before they have even met them.

"I took my young son Charlie along with me when I went to talk to Forest. He was three years old at the time. I signed for Forest, was delighted to do so, but then Mr Clough bought Charlie a toy tractor, a football and a cricket set. It was a lovely gesture.

"Even though I cost Forest £2 million I didn't really feel under much pressure to prove myself in Division One. People seemed to forget that I had already played there for Millwall, so it wasn't as if it was a new experience.

"I wasn't giving myself any time to re-adjust from Divison Two to Division One, I felt I had been quite successful when there with Millwall. I'd proved I could do it at the top level.

"Although my form in that first season was alright, it wasn't as good as it had been during my last campaign at the Den. I was pleased with the results the team were getting, but not necessarily with my own form.

"But I think that was down to the fact that the Forest way of doing things is different to Millwall's. The football Forest play is well known and respected throughout the League, but it can take some adjusting to.

"At first it was difficult. I was learning a new style of play during matches. But as the time went on I got more used to things. I could feel myself getting the hang of the system.

"Winning through to two cup finals in my first year really was the realisation of a dream. Everyone wants to play at Wembley and I was no exception."

Teddy's Wembley trips provided both agony and ecstasy as he experienced winning and losing underneath the world famous Twin Towers. Victory came against Southampton in the Zenith Data Systems Cup, while defeat reared its ugly head in the Rumbelows Cup showdown against Manchester United.

"Two finals in my first season, that's why I jumped at the chance of joining Forest. They aren't one of the biggest clubs in the country but they do enjoy great cup success.

"I really enjoyed my first year at the club," ends Teddy.

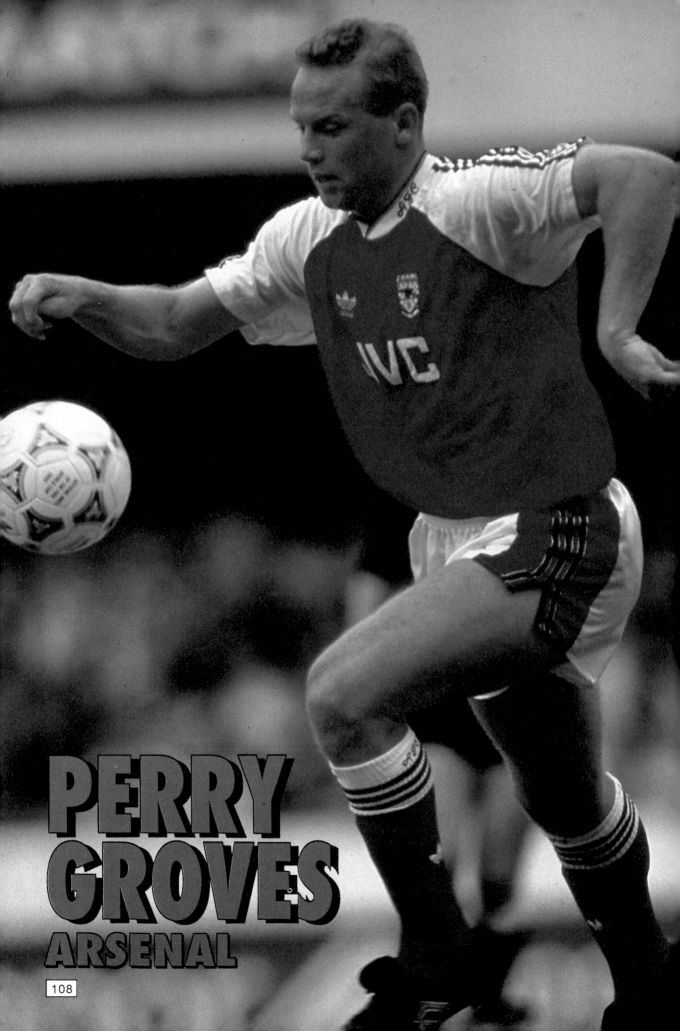

PERRY GROVES
ARSENAL

DAVID WHITE
MANCHESTER CITY

IT'S ALL CHANGE . . .

for Everton's MARTIN KEOWN

DAVE WATSON

HAVING made my England debut against France at Wembley last season, I lined up for my second full cap in Prague. Facing the Czechoslovakians alongside me was Arsenal's David Rocastle.

It was David's 12th outing in the white jersey. He'd made his England debut three years earlier on the strength of helping Arsenal win the League Championship.

Captaining the Highbury outfit that year and when Arsenal won the title again in 1991 was Tony Adams. He has 19 England matches behind him and won his first cap five years ago.

The connection is that I played alongside both David and Tony for Arsenal's youth team in the early 80's and we progressed into the first-team together. However, at 19-years-old, I chose to leave Highbury and thus missed their successful era.

However, I never once lost my self-belief as I moved from Arsenal to Aston Villa and then onto Everton. Despite the high profile my former team-mates were enjoying as championship winners, I refused to give up my belief that one day I would emulate their appearance in a full England team.

I reckoned that if I was good enough to play alongside them for Arsenal then I couldn't see why I couldn't match them on the international stage.

I have been through a lot of trials and tribulations since I chose to leave Highbury in the summer of 1986. But lining up alongside David Rocastle in Prague proved that I was right not to let the knockbacks I've had ruin the belief in my ability to reach the top.

Looking back I was too hasty in leaving Arsenal. It was over a contract dispute with manager George Graham. Perhaps the best decision I could have made then was not to have made one at all!

Instead I moved on to Aston Villa. Unfortunately for me, in my first season at Villa Park we were relegated to the Second Division. At the same time my old mates at Arsenal were lifting the Littlewoods Cup at Wembley against Liverpool.

I did reflect at that stage that it could have been me out there winning a medal and not heading for relegation. That was the time that my decision to leave Highbury hurt the most.

But I couldn't afford to let those regrets bother me for too long. I got on with my own game after that. I had too many other things to worry about to concern myself with Arsenal all the time.

I helped Aston Villa regain their First Division status the following season under Graham Taylor, who'd taken over at the club. He impressed me from the moment he walked into Villa Park and told all the players that we would definitely be promoted that season. You just had to believe him . . . and

he was right! He did a fantastic job.

But the fact he'd done so well and I was so impressed with him as a manager was one of the reasons I decided to leave Villa!

That might sound strange, but when Villa wanted me to sign a long term contract I figured that Graham Taylor wouldn't be at the club long term and that without him I reckoned Villa could well end up on the slippery slope down the division.

Anyone who'd worked with Graham Taylor realised that he'd go on to better things. I never had any doubts at that stage that in the near future he would be England manager.

On the strength of that I decided to leave Aston Villa and join Everton. It wasn't the happiest of times for me initially at Goodison. I was in and out of the side under Colin Harvey. I couldn't break the defensive partnership of Kevin Ratcliffe and Dave Watson.

I was so disillusioned there were times when I thought about asking for a transfer. I was so out in the cold at the club I might as well have been at the North Pole!

Then Howard Kendall rejoined the club as manager and I hoped for better things. However, one of the first things he said when he came back was that Ratcliffe and Watson were as good as when he left Everton in 1987 . . . and they were League Champions then!

That acted as a spur to me. I was determined to prove that I was as good as they were. However, I did have it in my mind that if I hadn't made a breakthrough by the end of that season then even if I hadn't asked to go, Everton would have probably been looking to get rid of me.

Fortunately, I did make the breakthrough. The manager played me in a five-man defence with Ratcliffe and Watson and then the significant moment came when he chose me ahead of Kevin for the

Zenith Data Systems Cup Final against Crystal Palace at Wembley in a back four formation. That was a turning point for me.

Less than a year later I was back at the stadium as an Everton regular making my England debut against France. It capped a remarkable change round in my fortunes.

KEVIN
RATCLIFFE

PAUL ELLIOT
CHELSEA

IT HAPPENED LAST SEASON . . .

Test your memory of 1991-92.

1. Which QPR striker became the first of the famous Allen footballing family to score a goal for England at any level?

2. There were only two ever-presents for Wales. Can you name them?

3. Which team spent the whole season in the Division's promotion race, went to Wembley twice and still ended the campaign with nothing?

4. Who beat both League Champions Leeds United and runners-up Manchester United by the same 4-1 scoreline?

5. Which Scots striker scored 18 goals for Bolton Wanderers after joining them from Celtic in January?

6. Who finished bottom of the Football League in 92nd place?

7. Name the Dutch defender who made an impact in Manchester City's team after joining them from Dordrecht?

8. Three Czech goalkeepers played League football in England. Can you name them and their clubs?

9. While the season was actually going on, which player was involved in the biggest transfer? Also, can you name the teams involved and the fee?

10. Who finished up as Manchester United's leading scorer?

11. Which Scottish club reached a Hampden final, but were also relegated?

12. Which club knocked Manchester United out of the FA Cup?

13. What piece of history did Rotherham United's Mark Todd create in the FA Cup first round replay against Scunthorpe?

14. Who scored the winning goal for Nottingham Forest in the Zenith Data Systems Cup Final against Southampton at Wembley?

15. Name the English-born manager who led Dundee to the Scottish First Division championship?

16. Gary Lineker scored in his last League match in England before his summer move to Japan. Who were the opposition?

17. At which London ground did Charlton Athletic play their home matches?

18. Which club did former England goalkeeper Peter Shilton become manager of?

19. Name the three clubs beaten in the promotion play-off finals at Wembley.

20. Who was the leading goalscorer in the Football League?

21. Which ex-Ranger rejoined the Ibrox club in a £1.3 million transfer?

GARY LINEKER — see question 16.

ANSWERS ON P 124

113

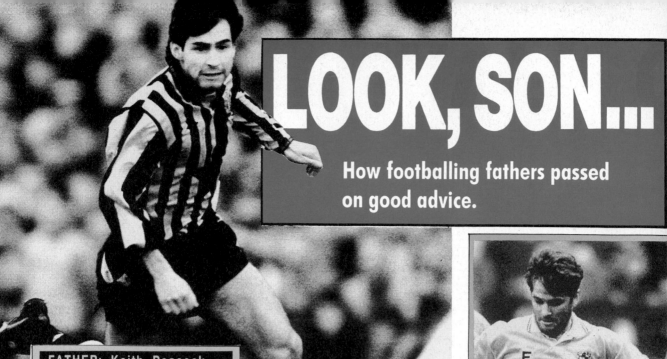

LOOK, SON...

How footballing fathers passed on good advice.

FATHER: Keith Peacock — Charlton midfielder.
SON: Gavin Peacock — Newcastle United midfielder.

GAVIN: "My father has given me a lot of good advice over the years, but probably the best tip he gave me was to work hard. He's seen players with a lot of talent who have gone to waste because they didn't work hard enough at their game. It's important to make the most you can out of your career.

"When I was just getting started he watched me all the time. He was really pleased when I got picked for England schoolboys. He never criticises, but he picked out areas of my game where I needed to improve and gave me bags of encouragement."

FATHER: Don Megson — Sheffield Wednesday and Bristol Rovers full-back and manager.
SON: Gary Megson — Manchester City midfielder.

GARY: "I think it can be harder for you to make your own name when your father has played in the game, although Nigel Clough is an example of how it can be done.

"When I left school my dad was manager of Bristol Rovers. I could have joined him there but we both thought it would be better if I went elsewhere. That way he could never be accused of playing me just because I was his son.

"Instead I went to Plymouth as an apprentice and I've never regretted it. I pretty much learned by my own mistakes. Because my dad was so busy in his own career he didn't get the chance to watch me play as often as most fathers would have liked.

"But he's been a great help when it comes to contracts. He's been on both sides of the manager's desk, so he knows all the ins and outs. As a result I've never needed an agent — and another bonus is dad doesn't want ten percent!"

FATHER: Tommy Wright — Sunderland, Oldham and Scotland outside-right.
SON: Tommy Wright — Leicester forward.

TOMMY JNR: "The main piece of advice my dad gave me when I became interested in football was to always be confident in my own ability. Everyone has their bad days in this game and he taught me you just have to believe in yourself.

"I think like a lot of footballing sons I wanted to follow in my dad's footsteps. He never pushed me into the game, but he always came to watch me when I was playing.

"But he can't believe the kind of wages footballers can get nowadays because it was a lot different in his day. He thinks we're all overpaid!"

FATHER: John Morrissey — Liverpool, Everton and Oldham winger.
SON: John Morrissey — Tranmere winger.

JOHN JNR: "I don't think there's one definite piece of advice my dad gave me. It was more a case of different tips he passed on over the years. I suppose the main thing he told me was to take care of myself. He taught me the importance of not abusing your body by smoking or drinking.

"I was offered trials at Everton, probably because dad had played with them, so you could say I owe my first big break to him. Mind you, I hope it was down to my ability alone when they offered me an apprenticeship!

"It's every boy's dream to become a professional footballer and probably every father wants that for his son. My dad was no exception and he and the rest of my family have always been very supportive."

FATHER: Brian Miller — Burnley player and manager.
SON: David Miller — Stockport midfielder.

DAVID: "Since I was young becoming a footballer was all I ever wanted to do. Before I could walk I was kicking a ball. It's in my blood and, like any father would, mine encouraged me to do what I wanted. He told me to give it my best shot. Of course you have to have some talent but it certainly helped having a dad with his amount of experience in the game.

"He taught me all the little do's and don'ts of being a professional and throughout my school years he encouraged me and passed on his knowledge by giving me tips here and there. He was a big help to me."

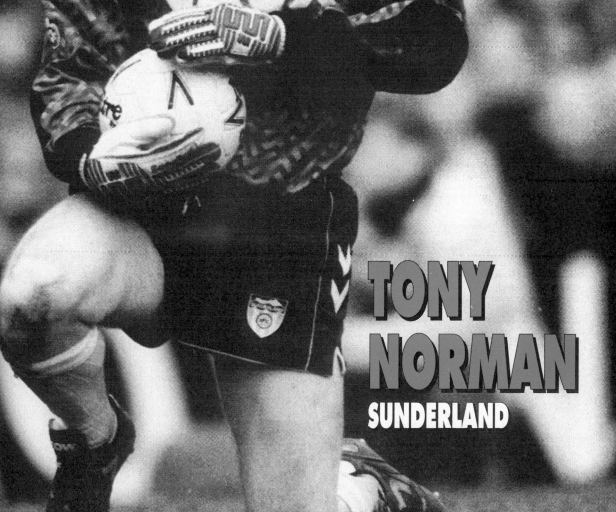

TONY NORMAN
SUNDERLAND

MATTHEW LE TISSIER

SOUTHAMPTON

These hands will stop anything.

'BORO'S BIONIC MAN!

IT was celebration time for Middlesbrough last season as they clinched promotion to the Premier League with a hard-fought 2-1 victory at Molineux on the final day of the campaign.

One player who celebrated more than most was goalkeeper Steve Pears. He knows that he's lucky to be playing top class football at all. After the injury problems he's had to overcome, he's the nearest thing the English League has got to a bionic man!

When he was only ten years old, Steve lost the top middle finger of his right hand after trapping it in a door. As you'd expect, that was very painful, but what was worse for a football-daft kid was that it could have meant curtains for his prospects of making it as a professional footballer when he grew up.

Steve soldiered on. With one finger shorter than it should be, he solved the problem of the "unused" finger of his glove flopping around by folding it over and taping it down. Maybe he could have got a discount on his

goalkeeping gloves!

One problem solved, but there were more to come. A couple of seasons ago, Steve injured the little finger of the same hand — thanks to his then team-mate Ian Baird!

It was a simple accident in training. As Steve dived for the ball at Ian's feet, boot made contact with finger, and Steve's little finger bent right back to touch his wrist!

It was back to hospital for Steve and bad news when the doctor looked at the shattered finger joint and told him that the chances were he'd never play again.

Doctors aren't always right, though, especially when they're dealing with stubborn characters like Steve Pears, who was determined to put himself back in the footballing frame.

After the bones of his finger were pinned together, he slogged his way through long and painful sessions of physiotherapy three or four times a week until he could finally put

on his goalkeeper gloves again. But they were gloves with a difference, now with two of the fingers strapped together.

A close-up of a very special pair of gloves.

Incredibly, Steve's injury problems didn't end there. He'd been having problems with his heel for four or five years, caused by spending lots of time on his toes as he stretched for dangerous crossballs or took off for a spectacular save.

In the end, Steve's heel became so painful that he could hardly get out of bed in the morning and had to walk downstairs sideways!

The answer was to have custom-built insoles made for his boots by a specialist, which meant Steve having both his feet put into plaster so that moulds could be taken.

They worked brilliantly. Steve is now playing superbly for the Ayresome Road club, but with finger and heel injuries behind him, don't anybody suggest that injuries always come in threes!

117

WALK ON!

The story behind a heart-warming day at Wembley

Proving that helping out a good cause is fun!

THE famous footballing chant "Walk On! Walk On!" took on a whole new meaning when the famous Wallace brothers of Manchester United and Leeds United fame launched one of the biggest charity events the game has ever seen.

Neither Manchester United nor Leeds United made it to last season's F.A. Cup Final, but for Rod and Ray of Leeds and Danny of Manchester United, it was an occasion to enjoy — the culmination of a huge publicity and fund-raising drive on behalf of sufferers of the crippling disease Multiple Sclerosis.

The Wallace brothers organised a campaign called 'National Football Against Multiple Sclerosis', which had as its centrepiece charity walks which ended at the F.A. Cup Final at Wembley and the Scottish Cup Final at Hampden on May 9, 1992.

The campaign's main aims were to raise money and awareness of the charity, 'Action and Research for Multiple Sclerosis' (ARMS), which offers self-help and a range of therapies for MS sufferers.

MS is the most common disease to hit the central nervous system. It affects an estimated 100,000 people in Britain and for most of those who suffer it's a life sentence. There is no known cure.

According to Rod Wallace, the campaign is the brainchild of brother Danny.

Rod says, "Danny had a little charity he started up in Southampton when he was still with the south coast club. He raised money to buy televisions for the local children's hospital.

"When the fund-raising finished on that project, he looked around for something a bit bigger. He met Anita Best, the chairperson of ARMS, and decided to help raise money for MS sufferers.

"Although he soon moved to Manchester United, he kept his involvement in the charity and it was at this time that my other brother Ray and myself became interested in helping Danny in his fund-raising activities.

"I have to admit I didn't know what MS was until I got involved with the charity. It's not one of the most publicised disabilities and hopefully what we're doing will bring it to the attention of more and more people."

The centrepiece of the appeal was three simultaneous fund-raising walks which began at the start of this year and took in a total of 131 Football League clubs in England and Scotland.

Two of the walks set off from London. These were the Western from White Hart Lane, and the Southern from Selhurst Park. The Eastern set off from Pittodrie

DANNY WALLACE

ROD WALLACE

WALK ON!

The long walk ended at Wembley!

Stadium in Aberdeen.

The Western and Southern walks ended at Wembley Stadium and the Eastern at Hampden. It proved to be a tremendous success for the organisers.

"It was a great occasion for everyone who is connected with the fund raising," Rod adds. "There were 100 walkers at Wembley Stadium wearing the colours of most of the Football League clubs. Most of these people were disabled and supported the team whose shirts they wore at Wembley. They were allowed to walk around the running track at the famous ground and received a tremendous reception from both the Sunderland and Liverpool fans.

"Everyone has been so co-operative," Rod goes on. "All the clubs agreed to provide players to go on the walks.

"Obviously, you can't ask players to do the complete walk from one club to another, so they did a couple of miles each.

"I was down on the south coast on the walk between Southampton and Portsmouth. It was great to see players from both clubs come together and do a few miles each for the charity."

One of the main ideas of the charity is the 'Wallace Wishline'. MS sufferers write in their soccer wish, and Rod, Ray and Danny try

to make it come true.

Rod continues, "One wish Ray and I helped to organise last season was that of an MS sufferer in the Leeds area who was unable to get to the ground.

"Myself, Ray and Gordon Strachan hired a couple of Rolls Royces, picked up him and his friends, and took them to Elland Road. We showed him round the dressing-room, where he chatted to the players.

"PROUD TO BE A FOOTBALLER."

"The whole thing was worthwhile, just watching the delight on the kid's face. I actually met the boy a couple of months later and he was still talking about his day at Elland Road.

"Events like these highlight the sort of problems that do exist at football grounds. For some disabled people it may be the only chance they get to see the players because clubs often don't have the facilities at grounds on match days to cater for special needs.

"Indeed, part of our aim must be to eventually get all clubs to recognise the need to have facilities for disabled as well as able-bodied fans.

"We had hundreds of organisers spread throughout the country helping us run the charity.

"Basically, we received a phone call from them requesting us to do something and we went out and did it.

"Some of the events I attended included a dinner in Huddersfield and a parade and other sideshows in Luton.

"Other events spread over a few months included lottery ticket sales and a 5-a-side football competition which had its final played at Wembley on FA Cup Final day. There was also the Great Footballoon Race, which required blowing up huge latex balloons publicising ARMS."

There was also an all-comers Subbuteo competition, a charity fashion show with players from Swindon Town strutting down the catwalk and a sponsored cycle ride from Manchester to Southampton.

Another big fund-raising effort was the 'Nationwide Football Against MS Week' at the end of April. The main event of the week was the 'Mayday Soccer Challenge' which had people showing their support for ARMS by getting sponsored to spend the day dressed as footballers.

"It was great to see footballers from all clubs up and down the country come together on such a positive note and help people who are less fortunate than ourselves. In fact, it made me proud to be a footballer!" Rod ends.

NIALL QUINN

MANCHESTER CITY

DREAMS COME TRUE!

EVERY football fan dreams of stepping on to the pitch at their favourite ground, running rings around the opposition and then topping it all by ~~ting~~ a screamer past the despairing arms of the 'keeper into the ~~ba~~ of the net!

Or maybe your dream is a bit more down to earth and you'd settle ~~for~~ a visit behind the scenes and a chat with your favourite players. For Preston fans, dreams like these really can come true!

Since joining the club in May last year, Commercial ~~Ma~~nager Paul Agnew has worked hard to make Deepdale ~~a k~~id-friendly zone.

After reporting the club's successes and failures for the ~~loc~~al Press and radio over a number of years, he knows ~~tha~~t the only way for Preston — first-ever ~~cha~~mpions of the Football ~~Le~~ague in 1889 — to recapture ~~pa~~st glories is to persuade a ~~wh~~ole new generation of fans ~~tha~~t Preston are the team to ~~wa~~tch on a Saturday afternoon.

~~I~~n December last year, Paul ~~lau~~nched the "Pick-Me-Up" ~~sc~~heme. It's a first in English ~~foo~~tball and gives the chance of ~~a li~~fetime to anybody under sixteen ~~wh~~o has suffered serious problems ~~an~~d deserves a "pick-me-up". ~~A~~nybody who knows a youngster ~~wh~~o has had an accident, been ill ~~or~~ suffered some kind of personal ~~tra~~gedy can get in touch with the ~~clu~~b and nominate him or her.

Commercial manager Paul Agnew — he knows that the future of the club lies with the kids.

Photograph   courtesy of Preston North End.

One of the first kids to benefit from the scheme was twelve-year-old Nigel Greenwood. He was badly burned when he fell against an electric cable on a railway line, so a Preston Pick-Me-Up was just what the doctor ordered! Especially when Nigel met one of his favourite Preston stars, namesake Nigel Greenwood!

Hope manager Les Chapman is watching. Maybe he'll sign me up!

YOU GET THIS!

Here's what's on offer for the lucky few who are ~~inv~~ited along to the ground, apart, of course, from the ~~ch~~ance to see the "Lilywhites" in action!

The Pick-Me-Up scheme includes —
Viewing the game from a luxury Executive box.
Refreshments.
The chance to see behind the scenes at the stadium.
Meeting the players.
Going home with a souvenir of their big day out.

~~After "training's~~ ~~ov~~er, it's time to ~~cle~~ar up — or ~~ma~~ybe this ~~gr~~oundsman is ~~dr~~eaming of ~~sin~~king a putt on ~~the~~ 18th green in ~~the~~ British Open ~~at~~ nearby Royal ~~Ly~~tham!

All in all it's a fantastic package and Preston are to be congratulated on their initiative, but the club's involvement with youngsters doesn't stop there.

They're only too willing to invite groups of kids along to the ground to have a look around, do some training on the pitch — and best of all, have a go at scoring a goal at the away end!

It's the kind of thing most kids dream about, but one thing's for certain, at Preston — dreams can come true!

JIM'S WAS JUST

for Rangers' kee

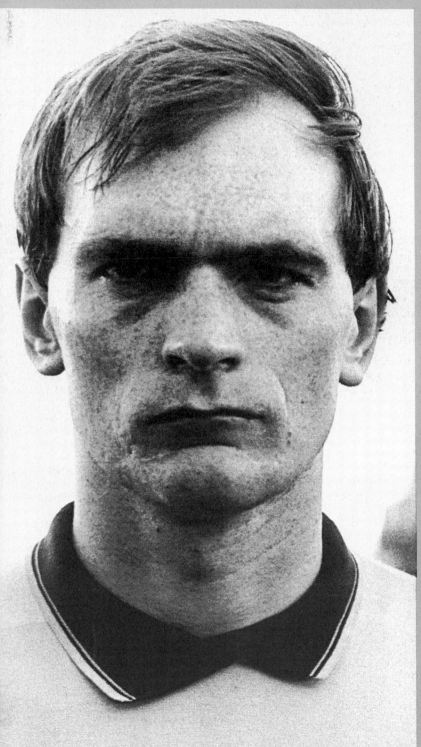

JIM LEIGHTON

ONE of the most pleasing aspects of this season fo. me has been Jim Leighton's return to top-flight action with Dundee.

Jim has been a real pal of mine ever since we teamed up with the Scotland squad seve years ago. The fact we have both been through thick and thin at club level has made us even greater friends.

For example, when I was being slated and finding it hard to settle during the early days of my Rangers' career, Jim was the first man on the telephone to give me the benefit of his experience.

He went through similar problems towards the end of his time at Old Trafford and his advice proved invaluable. He told me to get my mind sorted out and to distance myself from as many off-the-field distractions as possible.

Therefore, for starters, I stopped talking to the Press. I didn't want to start defending myself through the papers as that would probably have made things worse.

In retrospect, I think it was probably the right decision as everything is going well at Ibrox now too.

I know Jim as well as anyone and I can relate to the problems he had to suffer at Manchester United.

I'm delighted to see him back in the Premier Division. And I'm sure he'll be hoping to use his latest spell in the limelight to further his international claims.

When he arrived at Dundee last season, I genuinely believed he could be a real challenger for my Scotland jersey.

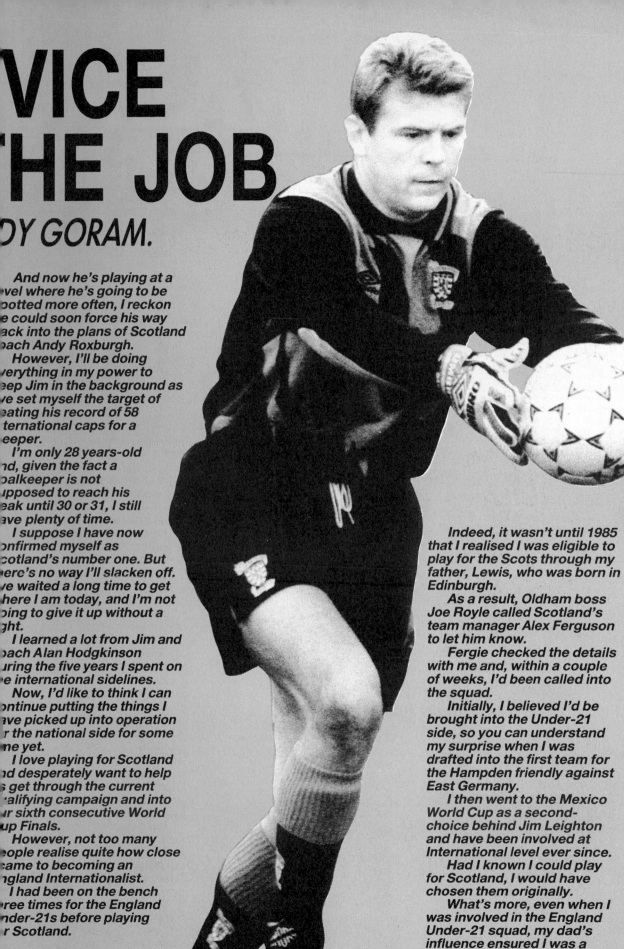

VICE
THE JOB

DY GORAM.

And now he's playing at a vel where he's going to be potted more often, I reckon e could soon force his way ack into the plans of Scotland oach Andy Roxburgh.

However, I'll be doing verything in my power to eep Jim in the background as e set myself the target of eating his record of 58 ternational caps for a eeper.

I'm only 28 years-old nd, given the fact a oalkeeper is not upposed to reach his eak until 30 or 31, I still ave plenty of time.

I suppose I have now onfirmed myself as cotland's number one. But erc's no way I'll slacken off. e waited a long time to get here I am today, and I'm not oing to give it up without a ght.

I learned a lot from Jim and oach Alan Hodgkinson uring the five years I spent on e international sidelines.

Now, I'd like to think I can ontinue putting the things I ave picked up into operation r the national side for some me yet.

I love playing for Scotland nd desperately want to help s get through the current alifying campaign and into ur sixth consecutive World up Finals.

However, not too many eople realise quite how close ame to becoming an ngland Internationalist.

I had been on the bench ree times for the England nder-21s before playing r Scotland.

Indeed, it wasn't until 1985 that I realised I was eligible to play for the Scots through my father, Lewis, who was born in Edinburgh.

As a result, Oldham boss Joe Royle called Scotland's team manager Alex Ferguson to let him know.

Fergie checked the details with me and, within a couple of weeks, I'd been called into the squad.

Initially, I believed I'd be brought into the Under-21 side, so you can understand my surprise when I was drafted into the first team for the Hampden friendly against East Germany.

I then went to the Mexico World Cup as a second-choice behind Jim Leighton and have been involved at International level ever since.

Had I known I could play for Scotland, I would have chosen them originally.

What's more, even when I was involved in the England Under-21 squad, my dad's influence ensured I was a Scotland supporter.

IT'S A FUNNY GAME . . .

. . . two stories from abroad that bear that out!

ROBBED BY THE REF!
claims Swansea's REUBEN AGBOOLA

MY father was born in Nigeria so I'm qualified for the national side.

I've found the game in Africa is totally different to anything you'll find in Europe.

For a start, it's difficult just getting from A to B because the roads are terrible. There are potholes everywhere and the volume of traffic is horrendous.

On some days the overcrowding gets so bad that you're not allowed to use the roads if the registration plate on your car starts with a certain number! One day it'll be odd numbers and the next it's evens.

Obviously, Nigerian attitudes are different too. Footballers are rich in comparison to the rest of the country but they're expected to look after hundreds of relatives.

I had to hand out money and clothes on behalf of my dad, even though I'd never seen any of these people before in my life!

Nigerian supporters are fanatical. For every international game there are crowds of 50-60,000. That's why it was awful to go out in the semi-final of the African Nation's Cup to Ghana.

All the players felt we were robbed. Before the game we discovered the match official was a Tunisian referee who Nigeria had had trouble with before.

Sure enough, his decisions went against us every time. In the end he gave Ghana a penalty for handball and we lost 2-1. But a BBC crew, who were filming over there, let me watch the incident again and again and I couldn't see a hand used at all!

Unbelievably, the next day the same referee was banned for five years! The crazy thing was that the result still stood so we were out of the tournament.

PRE-MATCH RITUAL WAS A SHOCKER
IAN WILSON looks back on his spell in Turkey.

WHEN I joined Turkish First Division Besiktas they had an open night on the eve of a new season.

The Turks have a traditi of slaughtering an animal before an important match one minute there was a sheep grazing on the touchline, the next minute they were cutting its throat

Those who carried out killing then dipped their hands in the blood and rubbed it on the players' boots and heads!

I started to walk off. didn't want to have anything to do with But the locals were offended, so I had sc blood smeared on n boots.

The Turks are fanat football followers. Wh we played Malmo in th European Cup in Istanl it was an 8 o'clock kick-

The stadium, which ho about 40,000 was full at 2 o'clock!

You couldn't see a thing for the first ten minutes of game because of smoke fr fireworks!

There are cheerleaders each section of the ground keep the chanting going. Being a cheerleader in Turkey is a profession! On guy was really proud to sh me his passport with 'National Cheerleader' entered alongside 'occupation'!

YOUR PICTURE GUIDE
ACTION! COLOUR!

PIN-UPS!

Printed and Published in Great Britain by D.C. THOMSON & CO., LTD., 185 Fleet Street, London EC4A 2HS.
© D.C. THOMSON & CO., LTD., 1992.
ISBN 0-85116-540-0

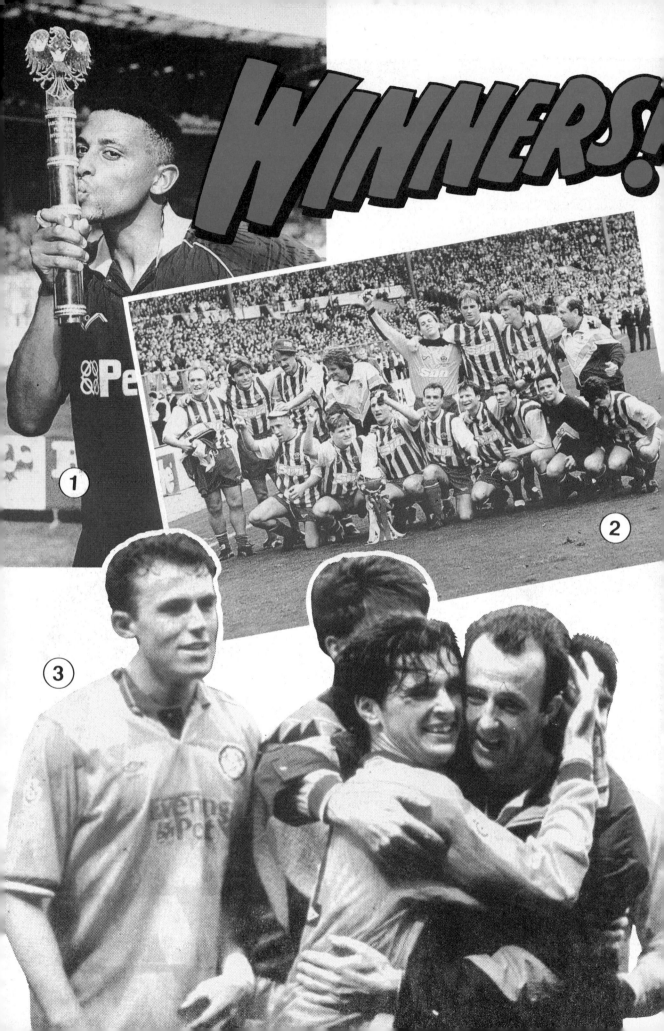

WINNERS!

1

2

3